Fifty Years of Wicca

Frederic Lamond
(Robert)

Green Magic

This edition is published by

Green Magic
Long Barn
Sutton Mallet
TA7 9AR
England

Typeset by Academic + Technical, Bristol
Printed and bound by Antony Rowe Ltd, Chippenham

Cover design by Chris Render

Cover production by Tania Lambert

ISBN 0 9547 2301 5

GREEN MAGIC

CONTENTS

ACKNOWLEDGEMENTS

I should like to thank all those who have given their time to read this manuscript, correct mistakes and suggest improvements, especially the members of the FutureCraft Email group, Professor Ronald Hutton, Philip Heselton and Jean Williams.

ABOUT THE AUTHOR

Born in 1931 Frederic Lamond studied Economics at Cambridge and Planning at the University of Chicago. After 5 years in market research he joined the computer industry in 1960 and has worked as an independent consultant and lecturer from 1975 until 2003. During that period he travelled extensively throughout Europe and North America. He is married and has two children and five grandchildren from his first marriage. After 39 years in and around London he has lived in Austria since 1994.

A life long pantheist, Frederic Lamond was initiated in February 1957 into Gardnerian witchcraft (now called Wicca). He is also a member of the Fellowship of Isis, the Church of All Worlds and the Children of Artemis www.witchcraft.org and is on the Council of the Pagan Federation www.paganfed.org. During his professional travels he has met the leading European and American Pagans and Wiccans. He is also active in interfaith work and attended the Parliaments of World Religions in Chicago in 1993, Cape Town in 1999 and Barcelona in 2004.

Besides many articles in Wiccan and other Pagan publications he is the author of:

The Divine Struggle, published by Nemeton in 1990,
Religion without Beliefs, published by Janus Publishing, London, in 1997.

INTRODUCTION

2004 should be a red letter year for Pagans. In March it was 100 years since Aleister Crowley had the mystical experience in the Cairo Museum which inspired his *Liber Al vel Legis* and became the basis of his Thelemite philosophy. And in November it is 50 years since Gerald Gardner's *Witchcraft Today* took witchcraft reconstruction out of the small reclusive world of magical lodges and presented it to the general public, which led to the growth of what is now called the Wicca movement. Time for both the OTO and Wicca to take stock of their achievements and failures of the past 100 and 50 years respectively.

I have never been a member of the OTO, so I must leave to one of its members the task of assessing Crowley's legacy. But in August it is also 50 years since I met the Goddess in the arms of my first fiancée, which led directly to my February 1957 initiation in Gerald Gardner's presence into his only coven of the time. I have thus lived through almost the whole of Wiccan history and am probably – since the death of Doreen Valiente – the oldest continuously practising Wiccan alive today.

I am probably also the most widely travelled, since my former profession as lecturer on the computer industry enabled me to visit all Western European countries and many parts of North America in the last 30 years. In each country that I have visited I made contact with local Wiccans and other Pagans and now have many friends among them.

This does not make me an authority to anyone but myself, as Wiccans like most Pagans acknowledge no spiritual authorities other than their own experiences of the divine. But I am as entitled as any other Wiccan to relate my experiences in Wicca and express opinions about current practice. Should these opinions differ at times from those of other writers this does not necessarily mean that one or other of us is wrong. We all write on the basis of our experiences and these experiences can be as varied as life itself.

Unlike my earlier *Religion without Beliefs* this book is intended to be read primarily by Wiccan initiates of the 2nd and 3rd degree. Like Caesar's Gaul and many other good things it is divided into three parts. In the first I relate the most salient of my experiences in Wicca, especially the magical ones, so that readers may know from where I am coming, and the basis for the opinions I shall subsequently express.

In the second part I describe what I consider to be the Wiccan movement's main successes and failures in achieving its stated aims, and whether the roots of these can be found in our rituals or the manner in which we perform them. Finally in the final part I describe my Wiccan ideal, and the minor changes required in the symbolism of Book of Shadows rituals to achieve this.

This does not mean that I am trying to found a Robertian Wiccan tradition to stand beside the Gardnerian, Alexandrian, Algard, Central Valley, Dianic, Eclectic and other Wiccan traditions, as an American Gardnerian who contributes to a Web discussion group has suggested. I don't need to massage my ego in that way, and don't want to add to the inter-traditional barriers to sharing magical circles that exist in the United States.

I am appealing on the contrary to covens of all Wiccan traditions to experiment with some of my ideas and their own. Rigid ritual formalism and conservatism are the hallmarks of a decadent religion or spiritual movement, and at 50 Wicca is a bit young to be decadent already. Living traditions are ever ready to renew themselves in their search for spiritual efficacy: the 21st century and its many challenges calls for no less!

Wernberg, Austria, 2004

I

Experiences

1

THE ENCOUNTER WITH APHRODITE

I was the only child of parents who divorced when I was two years old. My father did not then have the means, nor my mother the inclination, to bring me up, so I was taken on by my forceful overprotective Jewish maternal grandmother. She overfed me on cakes, so that I was always too fat to run and play with other children. At the outbreak of World War II, she took me to French Switzerland, leaving my grandfather and mother behind in England.

As the little fat foreigner I was naturally an outsider and inclined to introspection. From the age of 12, I went out of school hours on long solitary country walks when my contemporaries would be playing. It was on these walks, in the marvellous countryside above Lake Geneva, that I first felt a sense of oneness with the Universe, the moon and stars above, the hills and trees around me, especially on full moon nights. I also felt closest to whatever power had brought all these wonders into existence, and now maintained the marvellous balance of Nature. I never felt anything of the sort in the cold rational Protestant churches, and only a faint whiff of it in the warmer more colourful Roman Catholic ones.

My grandmother never sought to indoctrinate me, except to say: "All religious dogmas are lies!" and Goethe's dictum: "Honour silently the ineffable!" Nonetheless, when I was 13, she sent me to Protestant catechism with the advice: "It is part of the cultural baggage of an educated European to know who Moses, Elijah, Jesus, Paul and all that crowd were. So learn what they have to teach you. As to whether you want to believe it, make up your own mind!"

The three ministers of the parish of St François in Lausanne were kind, gentle and well meaning men, who had the best interests of their flock at heart. They were fond of me, because I took their teachings seriously, unlike some of my cynical classmates. But despite their best endeavours I found the God of the Old Testament utterly repugnant.

Jesus was a much more sympathetic figure: the height of human goodness as one could imagine it! But I never could believe that he was any more divine than any other good man in history, nor grasp why his death on the cross and resurrection a day and two nights later should affect my soul's salvation one way or another. Nonetheless, at the age of 15 I wanted to belong, and so agreed to be confirmed, hoping it was enough to believe in the ethics of Jesus to call myself a Christian.

At 16 I returned to England and spent two years at an Anglican High Church public (i.e. private boarding) school. At the end of every Sunday service, we had to turn to the East and recite the Nicene or Apostles' Creed. I had to remain silent for the two-thirds of the Creed I did not believe. Finally, a year later, I recognised that one cannot take a religion on a cafeteria basis. Since I did not and had never believed in the core Christian tenets, I could not honestly call myself a Christian.

FIRST INTUITION

From school I went straight to Cambridge, and its intense evening social life. Even then, in the late 1940s, it already had an evangelical fundamentalist society – the Cambridge Inter-Collegiate Christian Union (CICCU, pronounced 'kick you' because of their intrusive proselytising methods). Two CICCU students canvassed me, and I engaged them in theological argument. One soon gave me up as a hopeless cause, but the other kept visiting me, more to unburden his soul and share his own unhappiness than in any hope of converting me.

He must have been either sexually or emotionally abused in his younger days – or else racked by guilt at some messy sexual experience – because his misogyny was so extreme as to be laughable. In his speech and his letters to me he said women were the root of all evil in the world. I felt sorry for him, but took the opposite side of the argument to try to broaden his mind.

One day, during a walk, I heard myself saying: "The Christian churches keep saying that 'God is Love'. So human love must be at least the reflection of divine love. What is the purest and most selfless form of love we find among us? Surely, it is the love of a mother for her child, and of many a woman for her husband. Because they are more capable of loving more selflessly and more deeply than us, surely women must be closer to God than we are!" I surprised myself with this thought, because I had not previously thought deeply about the matter. But the Goddess heard me, and remembered.

This remark was not based on any personal experience. I had grown up well before the sexual revolution, and had attended only boys' schools. Cambridge colleges were then segregated and there were only two women's colleges compared with a dozen or more men's. So I found it difficult to understand young women and to interest them in me. I graduated at the age of 21 without ever experiencing a deep relationship. At Cambridge, however, I had managed to sublimate my frustrated sexual energy into political activism for European federalism.

The heart cannot be denied for ever, and the time came when I found sexual frustration no longer bearable. So one evening, I sank to my knees and prayed earnestly to God that He let me meet a girl whom I could love and respect, and who would love me in return: without knowing it I had cast my first spell. The immediate effect was a state of inner peace and confidence, as a voice in my head said: "Have faith! She will come in due course. Meanwhile, just concentrate on your studies!"

MY FIRST LOVE

A few weeks later, I was preparing for a ball, when I felt that that night would bring me the companion I had prayed for. Yet the evening began inauspiciously. I found myself stuck with a girl of Rubenesque proportions whose conversation was as thick as her thighs, and whom it required the dexterity of a tank commander to manoeuvre around the dance floor. At midnight, I was prepared to call it quits when a group of fellow students suddenly appeared from a private ball with some local girls in tow. One of them, Mary, was unaccompanied so I danced with her for an hour before taking her home. She was as light, graceful and witty as my previous companion had been thick. When I awoke the next day, I was madly in love. One week and three dates later, she returned my love passionately.

For the two years that our engagement lasted, we were separated most of the time by my studies, but were in constant telepathic contact. Each of us always knew what the other was feeling, and these intuitions were invariably confirmed by the next letter. On one occasion, I fell out of love for a few hours and wondered what I saw in Mary. It didn't last long before I was again feeling passionate, and I had been careful not to write to her during these few doubting hours. Yet in her next letter, she wrote: "You have been having doubts, darling. I could feel it. Please don't make me suffer!"

When we met again during the next long vacation, it was Mary who took the initiative in making our relationship physical. I was totally unprepared and did not want to make her pregnant, so I restrained myself. As she climaxed, I was suddenly catapulted out of space and time into cosmic consciousness: I was all the males of all ages and species making love to all the females of all time, while around us all the other couples were watching us like bodhisattvas in a Tibetan mandala, nodding approvingly as if to say: "Well done! Welcome to the club!"

In my head, a gentle but strong feminine voice (not my partner's) was saying: "All the empires and political systems, all the dogmas, philosophies and ideologies that men have formulated since the dawn of history, put together weigh less in the divine scales than a single embrace of two young lovers, or a single smile on the lips of a new born infant as it gazes at its mother for the first time."

The next day, I felt in a state of pure grace, cleansed of all sin by Mary's love. I floated on Cloud Nine with Mary for ten days, but after we parted, the curse of the intellectuals reasserted itself, and I felt I had to analyse my experience. If there were divine powers, I felt I had just encountered one, but which one? Not the vengeful Jehovah of the Old Testament, nor his long-suffering crucified Son: apart from Theresa of Avila Christianity and mystical sexual experiences just don't mix!

So I immersed myself in books on sexual psychology on the one hand, comparative religion and religious history on the other. Their insights intersected at the description of the love goddesses of Ancient Babylonia and Greece. So it was Aphrodite Herself whom I had encountered in Mary's arms! So She is a real universal energy, not the lifeless idol described by Christian ministers. It was She who had brought me peace of mind when I prayed to God in my frustration, She who had brought Mary and me together, She who had taught us the reality of telepathy and who had finally opened my consciousness to Her cosmos during our first intimate embrace! This was my initiation at Her hands. which is the basis of my opinion of what the Great Rite should be in Wicca.

Interestingly this experience occurred in the summer of 1954, when Gerald Gardner's *Witchcraft Today* was already in print. It was also the same year that an Indian professor of Philosophy called Rajneesh became enlightened, which led him to open an ashram in Poona.

But the Goddess was also jealous and did not want me to marry a mortal woman until after I had fully dedicated myself to Her. At that time I was earning my living quite successfully side by side with my studies; but on the two occasions when we made plans to marry my earnings suddenly collapsed and I faced grave financial difficulties. On the second occasion Mary's nerves, already severely tested by her parents' opposition, snapped and she broke off our engagement six weeks before our planned marriage, though it took another 12 months of deep unhappiness on both sides before our telepathic link was finally broken.

THE PATH TO WICCA

Freed from having to pretend to be Christian, I could now pursue my quest for fellow worshippers of the great Goddess in earnest. The English anthropologist Gordon Rattray Taylor's book *Sex in History* alerted me to Margaret Murray's theory that the mediaeval witches were not a mere figment of Inquisitors' sadistic imaginations, but the survival of a country Earth Mother religion. (This theory has been refuted by recent historians, but at the time it seemed plausible.) So I started looking for books on witchcraft, and it did not take me long to find Gerald Gardner's *Witchcraft Today*. For all his presentation of witchcraft as an innocuous survival from the past, it contained enough hidden cues to ring all my spiritual bells.

So I wrote to Gerald Gardner and was invited to meet him at his London flat in Holland Park. That meeting was followed by others with the members of his first coven. During the third such meeting, Jack Bracelin, Gerald's Man Friday, told me and another candidate that we had been accepted by the coven and would be initiated at the coming February Eve festival.

When the blindfold was removed from my eyes, and I found myself in a dark incense-filled candle-lit cottage surrounded by naked figures, I felt again the presence of the same divine power whom I first encountered in Mary's arms. And when the acting High Priestess read *The Charge of the Goddess,* I felt this power welcoming me home!

2

GERALD GARDNER

The man who welcomed me to his Holland Park, London, flat in June 1956 was a very lovable unassuming old gentleman with a great sense of humour, an excellent raconteur with a fine feeling for the absurdities of human life. He had spent 30 years in the Far East, as a tea planter in Ceylon, then as a rubber planter in Malaya, and finally from 1921 to 1936 as a customs officer for the British colonial government in Malaya. If, I thought, he was at all typical of British colonial administrators of his time I could understand why so many Indians and Malayans remember their erstwhile British masters with such affection.

While hunting for smugglers as a customs official Gerald had made the acquaintance of the Sea Dayak tribe and witnessed some of their shamanistic healing rituals. Convinced similar knowledge was to be found in the English countryside he devoted himself to finding it on his return to England in 1936 and joined the Folklore Society.

In 1937 he joined an archaeological dig in Palestine, during which his team found evidence that in the 7th century BCE the Jews had a balanced duotheistic religion, in which their male god of Creation Jehovah was married to the goddess of fertility Asherah. During a visit to Cyprus in 1938 he had a vision of how the cult of Aphrodite came to ancient Cyprus from Phoenicia, which he related in his first novel *A Goddess Arrives*.

Moving to Hampshire in 1938 he joined the New Rosicrucian Theatre in Christchurch, a branch of the Rosicrucian Fellowship of Crotona. Three of its members belonged also to a witches' coven engaged in witchcraft reconstruction on the lines of Margaret Murray's theory in *The Witch Cult in Western Europe*. One of them whom he called "Dafo" thought she had known him in a previous life. They became close friends and she initiated him into the coven in December 1939, at which Gerald found "everything I had looked for all my life."

8

Two of the other members came from a family tradition (which means they had learned their magic from their parents) and Gerald convinced himself that they provided what he called the New Forest coven with a link with hereditary country witchcraft stretching back to the Middle Ages or even the Stone Age.★

With the enthusiasm of the new convert he wanted to publicise the coven's practices to gain more members, but its other members restrained him, holding him to his oath of secrecy. It was not until most of the other members had died off that he was allowed to describe their witchcraft practices in fictional terms in *High Magic's Aid*, published in 1948, and not until after the repeal of the 1734 Witchcraft Act by Parliament in 1951 that he was allowed to write the directly descriptive *Witchcraft Today* that was published in 1954 and which had brought me to him.

Gerald cultivated a somewhat demonic appearance with a narrow barbiche and by combing his white hair upwards on both sides to make them look like horns. But for a man claiming to revive the awesome mysteries of witchcraft I found him surprisingly lacking in charisma. Doreen Valiente, with whom I corresponded in later years, disagreed with me on this: she found him charismatic when she first met him in 1953.

ORIGIN OF WICCAN RITUALS

Forbidden by his fellow coven members from using their rituals with his new initiates, he borrowed his initiation and circle opening rituals from Freemasonry (to which he had belonged since 1909 at the age of 25) and the Greater Key of Solomon, because they sounded good and had lots of morphic resonance in Rupert Sheldrake's term. But he didn't bother to check whether the meaning of the words was in harmony with the spirit of Goddess worship. I was shocked during my initiation

---

★ Note: My sources for this version of Gerald's encounter with what was to become Wicca are:

1. Gerald Gardner's personal reminiscences during C&W chats.

2. The book *Gerald Gardner, Witch*, researched and written by Idries Shah on the basis of interviews with Gerald, but signed by Jack Bracelin.

3. *The Triumph of the Moon*, by Prof Ronald Hutton of Bristol University.

4. *Wiccan Roots*, by Philip Heselton.

5. *Gerald Gardner and the Cauldron of Inspiration*, by Philip Heselton.

when the ritual sword was presented with the words: "With this in your hands you can command angels and demons." Angels and demons, I thought, what are they doing in what is supposed to be a non–dualistic pantheist religion? Gerald must be theologically illiterate!

It wasn't the only contradiction. During the initiation one had to swear by one's hope of an afterlife to keep the Craft ever secret, but Gerald himself was keen to be interviewed on it by even the most questionable popular papers. It would have been so easy for him to say: "Experienced high priests and priestesses know what it is safe to say, and what should be kept secret, but new initiates without that experience should keep everything secret!" but he didn't feel the need to justify himself.

Attempts by the coven's older members to restrain him failed, and six weeks after my initiation the coven split, with the older members going off with Doreen Valiente, while Dayonis – who now became his High Priestess – Jack Bracelin, a young hospital anaesthetist, another new initiate and I myself stayed with Gerald.

AN UNASHAMED SENSUALIST

If an interview with the *Western Mail* in March 1957 was the occasion for the break between Gerald and the older coven members led by Doreen Valiente, it was not the root cause. Gerald was an unashamed and some-what innocent sensualist.

A lifelong asthmatic, he found the binding and scourging method the only one in which he could reach an altered state of consciousness, and he was absolutely obsessed with it. He introduced it not only into the initiation and 2nd degree elevation ceremonies – where it may have antedated him – but into a "purification" ritual at the beginning of each meeting, and into the method of raising power when working magic. When he himself was being scourged he kept on saying "Harder! Harder!" which was greeted with expressions of considerable distaste on the faces of several older members. And he introduced references to it at the beginning of the *Charge of the Goddess* and the consecration of the water and the salt.

By the time I was initiated in February 1957 the coven was meeting in a re-erected "witches' cottage" on the grounds of the Fiveacres nudist club which belonged to Gerald. Since meetings could last until fairly late members without cars or with long distances to cover slept in a hut neigh-bouring the witches' cottage. Gerald liked to cuddle up with whoever had been his high priestess: he was too old to engage in penetrative sex but would have enjoyed affectionate caresses.

Doreen Valiente found this embarrassing. Temperamentally monogamous she was also married to a very jealous Spanish husband who did not belong to the Craft. She obviously didn't inform him of the details of what happened at coven meetings – her oath of secrecy would have forbidden this anyway – but she must have imagined that any knowledge of cuddles with Gerald would have endangered her marriage. So she frequently stayed away from coven meetings: she was not present at my initiation and it was the Maid Dayonis who initiated me.

Dayonis had no such inhibitions. She had a very open relationship with Jack Bracelin and was temperamentally warm and affectionate. Cuddling up with her must have been much more enjoyable for Gerald than with the reserved Doreen, and he became very fond of her. Early in 1957 he wrote a letter to Doreen in which he stated that "according to the Laws of the Craft" there comes a time when an older High Priestess must hand over to a younger more nubile one.

This was an abuse of a tradition that the Beltane fertility ritual – and only that one – must be performed by fertile partners, and it is most unlikely that Doreen had already had her menopause in early 1957. That letter probably accounts for Doreen's absence from my initiation.

Gerald's wife Donna, a former nurse, did not belong to witchcraft but was very tolerant of his activities. According to Cecil Williamson (not the most reliable of sources) she said on one occasion: "I don't mind how many young women Gerald can get to whip him, as long as I don't have to be involved!"

AN UNBRIDLED IMAGINATION

Gerald's invocation of the "Ancient laws of the Craft" in his letter to Doreen suggesting she step down as High Priestess is only one example of a devious creative attitude to factual truth.

After the break Doreen's coven asked if they could continue to meet in the witches' cottage at the Fiveacres nudist club until they had found their own premises. Gerald could have replied: "The nudist club and the cottage are my property. If you are not prepared to circle with me anymore you can't circle on my property!" Instead he replied: "There is an ancient law dating back to the Burning Times" (a favourite expression of his) "that for security reasons no witch coven may meet less than 25 miles from another witch coven's meeting place."

The new High Priestess Dayonis had an elfine face that looked as if she had come straight out of an Arthur Rackham drawing. Gerald told reporters that she came from a hereditary witch family whereas her family were Armenian Jews living in Cardiff. Having learned from her a few more of Gerald's porkies I wondered a mere eight weeks after my initiation whether the old fraud had invented witchcraft altogether.

I had a tough three days before an inner voice told me: "It doesn't matter! The Craft works for you. The initiation rituals brought you into permanent spiritual contact with the eternal Goddess whom you first encountered in your first lover's arms, and the spells always seem to achieve the desired results. Does it then matter whether the rituals that brought you there are three or three thousand years old?" These doubts and the answer to them compressed into eight weeks what might have been ten years of spiritual development if Gerald had been a more credible teacher.

Thus reassured I speculated more calmly whether Gerald had invented the Craft or been initiated as he said into a pre-existing coven. I found the Wiccan system to have a depth and coherence that I did not find in Gerald, unless he was hiding his light under a bushel to force us to think for ourselves. Dayonis and Jack Bracelin also visited Dafo subsequently, thus confirming her existence. More recently thorough research by Ronald Hutton and Philip Heselton has also confirmed the existence of the Rosicrucian Fellowship of Crotona and of the New Forest coven.

Recently it has occurred to me that these factual lies might nonetheless have contained mythical truths. There almost certainly was no unbroken line of initiations from mediaeval – let alone Stone Age – country witches to our coven, but there was a link between them and us at the level of the collective human unconscious. And women like Dayonis, who looked the part of the magnetic young witch so well, might have owed their charisma to earlier incarnations as a priestess or shamaness. But what would a contemporary reporter know about the collective human unconscious and the belief in reincarnations?

Gerald Gardner was also a man of his times, and all esoteric movements of the late 19th and early 20th centuries were still influenced by the Christian belief that all truth is inherited from the past. The Freemasons, into whom Gerald had been initiated in 1909, claimed to trace their arcane knowledge to Hiram, the architect of Solomon's Temple, whereas speculative Freemasonry first arose in 16th century Scotland. René Guénon, the French esotericist, saw himself as a "priest in the Order of Melchisedek." And the founders of the Order of the Golden

Dawn claimed they had been given a charter to do so from a German Rosicrucian initiate – Fräulein Sprengel. No wonder Gerald or the New Forest coven felt they had to portray the witchcraft revival movement as in a long line of initiations.

WICCAN LINEAGE

The paradox is that Gardnerian witchcraft does indeed have an pedigree that is at least 3000 years old. By borrowing its rituals from Freemasonry and the Greater Book of Solomon, Gardner or the New Forest coven placed it in the descent from Renaissance Magic, which descended from 13th century Spain, which descended from the Sufis, and through them from the city of Harran (in contemporary Anatolia) and eventually from the magi of ancient Babylon. No wonder the rituals of the Book of Shadows have such morphic resonance.

But contrary to E. W. Liddell's *Pickingill Papers* edited by Michael Howard there is no evidence that Gerald Gardner ever met a genuine country wise woman or cunning man, nor did he claim to have done to his biographer Idries Shah. He did not know nor teach us any herbal lore, nor how to communicate with animals and influence the weather, which were and are the stock in trade of genuine country witches.

Neither Renaissance magicians nor country witches practised ritual nudity, at least not in groups. According to Charles Leland that was a Tuscan *strega* tradition from a country where the climate is rather more conducive to it. But apart from *Aradia, Gospel of the Witches* it was also in line with the whole English Progressive counter-culture movement of the first half of the 20th century, as Ronald Hutton has written in his *Triumph of the Moon*. At the time of my initiation I already belonged to the *Progressive League*, which promoted pacifism, European federalism, World Government, socialism, progressive (i.e. non-authoritarian) education, nudism and free love, and which had been founded in the 1930s by the writer H. G. Wells among others.

GERALD GARDNER'S TEACHINGS

Gerald Gardner spent summers at his Witchcraft Museum on the Isle of Man, but in the winter of 1957–58 he lived at his Holland Park flat and circled with our coven in Bricket Wood. After cakes and wine he used to tell us stories about what happened in "Pre-Burning times".

At the time I was rather cynical about these stories and thought to myself: "Good old boy! He is trying so hard to persuade us that there is a continuous tradition stretching back to the Middle Ages if not the Stone Age, whereas we all know that this is utterly unprovable, and that even today's family traditions might not go back further than the occult revival of the 1890s".

More recently I realised that he was using – consciously or unconsciously – a historical mirror image technique. When he was saying "This is what happened in Pre-Burning times" he really meant "This is what you should do when times have become sufficiently tolerant for you to emerge from the broom closet, go public, and acquire a lay following." Here then are some of his stories.

The Circle

"Ceremonial magicians draw a circle to keep out the spirits they summon. Witches draw a circle to keep the power we raise in!"

Spiritual Development

"If you concentrate on helping others, your spiritual development will take care of itself!"

The Book of Shadows (BoS)

"The Book of Shadows is not a Bible or Quran. It is a personal cookbook of spells that have worked for the owner. I am giving you mine to copy to get you started: as you gain experience discard those spells that don't work for you and substitute those that you have thought of yourselves." Sound advice, but it was inconsistent with his attempt to make its contents look centuries old, with advice on what to do if one was caught by witch-finders and tortured, as well as occasional phoney archaisms, such as: "Keep your book in your own *hand of write*" and "At *mine* altars. . ."

It bothered Gerald that we knew that he had put the Book of Shadows (BoS) rituals together with Doreen Valiente's help, because he dearly wanted us to believe they had an older provenance. So one day he told us with a sly look on his face: "Until recently witches were not allowed to write anything down, lest it incriminate them if their house was searched. When at last Books of Shadows were allowed, witches had to write their rituals and spells down in a jumbled manner, so that if any unauthorised person found the BoS and tried the rituals as written down they wouldn't work!"

Was he telling us he had deliberately jumbled up the rituals to force us to think about them critically and creatively? If so, he had overreached himself, because Dayonis and later high priestesses went strictly by the book and Gerald, when present, never turned a hair.

Intentionally or not there are, however, plenty of inconsistencies in the initiation and circle opening rituals, which could be ironed out without depriving the rituals of any of their morphic resonance. I shall suggest some of these in the third part of this book.

It is doubtful that he gave similar caveats to the three subsequent initiatory lines that he created. Hence the widespread belief among Wiccans descended from Eleanor Bone, Patricia Crowther and Monique Wilson that the BoS rituals do indeed have an ancient provenance.

Seasonal Festivals

"In Pre-Burning times the four great sabbaths" – Candlemas, Beltane, Lammas and Halloween is what we called them then before the Celtic authenticity craze of the 1970s – "were great big parties in which the whole village celebrated the end of one of the periods of hard work in the agricultural cycle. Only the full moon esbats were private for initiated witches because that is when spells would be cast. It is only the persecutions that have turned us into a priesthood without a congregation."

In line with this he encouraged us to invite any life affirming but not necessarily esoterically inclined friends to bonfire parties at the Fiveacres Club at the time of the four major seasonal festivals. The Regency, a rival witchcraft tradition founded by Robert Cochrane, held open rituals in the late 1960s, but it wasn't until the 1980s that American Pagans started open seasonal festivals and gatherings, and the 1990s that the UK Pagan Federation followed suit.

During the same session I asked Gerald why we celebrated the cross-quarter days instead of the solstices and equinoxes. "You can celebrate these if you want to," said Gerald, "but it would be at odds with the climate in which we live. You see: the most important festival in the witch year is the springtime fertility festival, when young couples would make love in the fields to stimulate crop growth. This could only happen when the nights had become warm enough to sleep out of doors.

"In the Eastern Mediterranean and Palestine this is soon after the Spring Equinox: hence the timing of the Jewish Passover which replaced the spring orgy after Moses. In Southern England, Holland and Germany it doesn't normally become warm enough to sleep out of doors until the beginning of May. Hence the popular ditties:

"Hurray, hurray for the first of May
Outdoor loving starts today!"

and

"Never cast a clout until the May is out!"

(the mayflower or white hawthorn).

"In Scandinavia it doesn't become warm enough for outdoor love-making until Midsummer, which is why 21 June is celebrated to this very day in Norway, Sweden and Finland with bonfires around which young people dance until dawn, with many couples disappearing into the bushes.

"During the spring fertility festivals a lot of young women, especially the May Queen, would become pregnant and their children would be born nine months later. That was therefore the right time to celebrate the birth of the new solar year: shortly after the winter solstice in the Mediterranean, but not until the beginning of February in Southern England, Holland and Germany."

With these words Gerald confirmed that the seasonal festivals are intended to make us more aware of the cycle of seasons in nature, and that their dates should therefore be determined by the climate in which we live – a lesson that witches in North America, South Africa and Australia should take to heart!

At the great sabbaths we used to have great feasts – often shared with non-initiated friends as I have already mentioned – whereas after full moon esbats we had only moon cakes and wine. We liked our feasts, so after Gerald's return to the Isle of Man in the spring 1958 we decided to celebrate both the cross quarter days and the solstices and equinoxes with feasts. Gerald did not object when he heard of it, since this brought us closer to his Druid friend Ross Nichols, who was about to secede from the Ancient Druid Order to found the Order of Bards, Ovates and Druids (OBOD).

The eight festivals were subsequently rationalised (I don't know by whom) as celebrating the eight spokes of the Celtic wheel of the year. Even Doreen Valiente, who should have known better, supported this interpretation in one of her books.

But the results were not entirely positive. As coven members didn't feel like meeting more than once a month on average, we ended up with eight seasonal festivals and five full moon meetings for casting spells, instead of 4 and 12 as previously. The first step had been taken in turning a spellcasting craft into a liturgical system.

AN OLD MAN IN A HURRY

Gerald believed firmly in reincarnation, and that initiates of the mysteries can choose the time and place of their next incarnation. He knew that he did not have long to live and wanted to be reincarnated into a witches' coven, but for that to be possible there had to be witches' covens around after his death. So as time went on, he watered down more and more of the very sensible requirements for initiation in order to maximise the number of witches that were initiated.

One requirement is that candidates for initiation must wait a year and a day between their request to join a coven and their actual initiation. Yet I was initiated only seven months after my first meeting with Gerald and four months after meeting the rest of the coven for the first time. At the time I thought they made an exception for me because of what I told them about my mystical experience of the Goddess two years earlier, but subsequent candidates were put through similar accelerated procedures.

After Gerald's break with Doreen Valiente, he sent all the inquirers' letters he received to Dayonis with instructions to initiate them as soon as possible. Some of the candidates posed no problems because they were temperamentally close to us; others were somewhat more doubtful but we initiated them nonetheless.

When Eleanor Bone came to visit us, however, we felt we could not circle with her. This was no reflection on her sincerity, but simply that she was substantially older, and her reserve as the responsible matron of a nursing home clashed with the exuberant gaiety of existing coven members. Gerald insisted that she be given a private 1st degree initiation. This done he took over her training and within a month had put her through the 2nd and 3rd degrees and installed her as the high priestess of a new line. If the degrees were supposed to represent stages in spiritual development, I felt this accelerated procedure made a mockery of them.

For the development of the Wicca movement, however, it was a master stroke of Gerald's. After his death in 1964 Eleanor Bone and Patricia Crowther were far more faithful to his aims than the Bricket Wood coven was. Whereas we had been scalded by unwelcome publicity (see the next chapter) and therefore kept ourselves to ourselves, initiating only companions and close friends of existing members, Eleanor and Patricia kept on giving interviews whenever requested, and became the public face of Gardnerian Wicca in the late 1960s and 1970s. Interested inquirers thus approached them and Eleanor Bone became the grand-mother of most Gardnerian Wiccans in the South of England, Patricia Crowther of those in the North.

Symbolic Rituals

Wicca is a craft in the mediaeval sense: a skill, that of casting mental spells to ask the Goddess and Horned God to help us and others. We can become much more proficient in this if we can transcend the mental and physical barriers with which we surround ourselves to protect our separate egos. In Wicca there are a number of radical rituals to challenge members' barriers and break them down.

One of these is ritual nudity and this is generally practised by all Gardnerian covens throughout the world. But most covens shrink from the other two and perform them only symbolically. Gerald initiated this trend with the Great Rite at 3rd degree elevation, and did not object when the ordeal at initiations and 2nd degree elevations was also practised symbolically.

Few if any High Priestesses thus achieved the degree of ego-transcendence that would have enabled them truly to channel the Goddess when the Moon is called down on them, but the lowering of the requirements undoubtedly helped the movement to grow faster.

IDRIES SHAH

In 1959 the charismatic Sufi grand master and writer Idries Shah appeared on the scene and took an interest in the Bricket Wood coven. He was wont to hold court for anyone interested in Sufism at a table in the Cosmo Restaurant in Swiss Cottage (North London) every Tuesday evening. Jack Bracelin attended these and was soon questioned by Idries about his background and interests. When he mentioned that he was the right-hand man to Gerald Gardner in the witchcraft revival, Idries asked to meet Gerald and then offered to interview him and write his biography. This duly came out in 1961 under the title *Gerald Gardner, Witch* but signed by Jack Bracelin because Idries did not want to confuse his Sufi students by being seen to take an interest in another esoteric tradition.

As he was coming to the end of his research Idries came one day to have tea with my wife Gillian and me, accompanied by his girl friend and Jack Bracelin. He seemed to have become somewhat disillusioned with Gerald because he said: "When I was interviewing Gerald I sometimes wished I was a *News of the World* reporter. What marvellous material for an exposé! And yet" – here he looked thoughtful – "I have it on good authority" (I assume he meant the inner planes) "that this group will be the cornerstone of the religion of the coming age. But rationally" – and here he looked despairingly at us sincere but by his standards woefully ignorant young people – "rationally I can't see it!" He also felt Gerald was driven by a power he didn't fully understand.

3

LIFE IN THE BRICKET WOOD COVEN

I had asked to join Gerald Gardner's coven for religious reasons: to worship the great Goddess of Life and Love together with others. But learning to cast spells was part of the package, indeed the witchcraft tradition's main purpose at the time.

At the first Full Moon meeting after my initiation, which was also the last before the coven split, Doreen Valiente as High Priestess asked: "Do we have any work to do?" Someone's friend was poorly and we resolved to help him regain his health and strength rapidly by means of a remote healing. His photo was passed around.

"What do I have to do?" I asked. "During the working just visualise this person being healthy and strong. If you find visualisation difficult, just give your power to X in the middle of the circle, who will be the transmitter."

In those days, binding and scourging was the only method we used for raising power, because it was the only one that worked for Gerald. The coven member who knew the person we were working for best knelt in the middle of the circle and was scourged by his or her partner while the rest of the coven just stood around them in a circle and contributed their power.

I soon found out that I was a very good power conductor. As soon as the working started I found myself hyperventilating at an ever faster rate, while also visualising which I didn't find difficult at all. When I tried breathing as fast outside the circle at home I nearly fainted from oxygen intoxication when I had reached barely a quarter of the speed with which I breathed during the raising of cones of power.

In the spring of 1958, after Gerald had left us to spend the summer on the Isle of Man, we decided that the B&S method of raising power was too damn boring. So we switched to the circle dance method of raising power, sometimes with a transmitter still kneeling in the centre of the

20

circle, sometimes without, as we all visualised the desired outcome while running around at an ever increasing speed. Someone mentioned that the Lakota Sioux dance for hours on end until they drop from exhaustion to raise power for their spells: we never managed more than 5 minutes at most, yet the spells still worked.

We also altered the "Purification" procedure at the opening of every circle. Whereas under Gerald each member was scourged individually by his or her partner while the rest of the coven looked on, we now decided all the men should be scourged simultaneously by their women partners, which was followed by all women being scourged simultaneously by their male partners.

Having experienced intense telepathy with my first love I had no difficulty believing in the possibility of remote healing as a form of purposeful guided telepathy, but I had no emotional commitment to its efficacy or lack thereof, and was therefore curious to see whether our spells achieved the desired results. They almost invariably did within a much shorter timespan than one would have expected if nature had simply taken its course. With each successful spell I approached the next spell with greater conviction and less scepticism.

On the other hand, I was hopeless at scrying and never mastered the art of divination for others, be it through laying a deck of Tarot cards, throwing Chinese coins or yarrow sticks to find the relevant set of trigrams from the I Ching, or learning to cast astrological horoscopes. But a few months after my initiation I had an interesting experience of precognition.

A CASE OF PRECOGNITION

On the grounds of the Fiveacres nudist club on which we met for our witch meetings, there were a number of sites on which the members who had rented them could place caravans or build cottages for staying over spring, summer and early autumn weekends. In September 1957 I bought an old (originally horse drawn) gipsy caravan from a couple who were moving away and lived there permanently for the next two years. I never felt lonely there, even during the winter months when no members came to the club. On the contrary when I returned from work in the evenings and opened the gate to the club grounds I was greeted by a rustle of leaves by the trees nearest the entrance.

I worked at the time at *The Economist Intelligence Unit* in Jermyn Street near Piccadilly, an early pioneer of flexitime which allowed us to work from 10 or 10.30 a.m. to 6.0 or 6.30 p.m. to avoid commuting in crowded rush hour trains. I would therefore normally leave my caravan shortly before 9 a.m. for the 15 minute walk to Bricket Wood railway station to catch the 9.17 shuttle train to Watford Junction, where I changed to a train for London. The shuttle was scheduled to arrive at Watford at 9.25, one minute after an express from Northampton was scheduled to leave on a non-stop run to Euston. That express was frequently a few minutes late and when it was I was able to catch it, thus reaching my office a good half hour earlier than if I had taken the slow Bakerloo Line train to Piccadilly.

For three weeks in December 1957, I knew when I left my caravan every weekday morning whether I would be able to catch the express at Watford Junction or not, and my certainty was invariably confirmed half an hour later at Watford. On three occasions I was unsure and found the express standing at its platform at Watford when the shuttle train pulled into the station. It was then a case of dashing as fast as possible down the stairs, through the subway and up the stairs to where the express was standing just as the guard blew the whistle to let the express leave. On one occasion I was able to climb on to the train as it was beginning to move, on the other two occasions it was already too fast and I had to let it go.

The Yule and New Year break then intervened. When work resumed in January I had lost the precognition of what would happen at Watford Junction. I tried to guess but the results were no better than the 50 percent random hit rate.

THE THEORY OF DIALECTICAL PANTHEISM

From the time of my initiation I was struck by the happy atmosphere of witch coven meetings, in which there is a lot of joking and fun beside the seriousness of spiritual healing and other spellcasting; which contrasts so strongly with the po-faced seriousness of Jewish and Christian worship.

Why then did the monotheistic religions fight so fiercely to eradicate Nature worship in the lands they controlled and persecute their adherents? Why did Christianity promote a dualist antagonism between the Spirit and the Flesh, with only the former conceived as in the "image of God"? Why was it so fanatical in its hatred of sexual pleasure, and the degradation of the social status of women?

I was pondering these questions a few weeks after my initiation. Shortly afterwards the answer came to me in a sudden flash of insight, much like many a scientific theory first appeared to its discoverer.

The evolution of the Universe and especially of life on Earth has been the product of a dialectical antagonism between two cosmic forces:

- The highly conservative power of **Love**, which seeks to maintain all living species and ecological equilibria just as they are at any given point in time, and is *immanent* in the genetically inherited instincts of all living species, including humanity. This is the power we invoke as the Goddess of Life and Love and her consort the Horned God of fertility, and which is also present in the many gods and goddesses of polytheistic ethnic religions.

- A force of **Destructive Creation**, which seeks forever to upset existing equilibria in order to force at least some of the existing species to become more highly evolved in order to survive. In a universe in which the total amount of energy is constant and can neither be added to nor reduced – although it can be converted to matter and back again – neither god nor man can create anything without destroying something else. This is the power the Jews call JHVH, the Christians God the Father, Muslims Allah and Hindus Shiva.

Both forces are aspects of the all-inclusive Ultimate Reality: neither is evil nor undesirable, although an imbalance between the two forces frequently is. If only the force of Love existed, the Universe would never have moved from its original state of undifferentiated Nothingness. It would be like the unchanging surface of the Moon where nothing ever happens. Significantly we call our Goddess also "our Lady of the Moon"

But if only the force of Destructive Creation existed, the whole Universe would be like the Sun: an endless series of thermonuclear explosions creating new elements, but which last only a few microseconds before dissolving again in the fiery furnace. The Sun plays an important role in many religions that worship the power of Creation, which are therefore often referred to as solar religions.

On Earth, on the other hand, there is an ongoing delicate balance between these two antagonistic cosmic forces. The result has been the slow process of Evolution on Earth in which continents, mountains, plants and animals have slowly appeared and individual plants and animals live actively long enough to experience their own life, but in which species can also slowly evolve over succeeding generations.

Until some 150 000 years ago the Destructive Creative force acted mainly from outside the Earth through asteroid impacts or sunspots and sunstorms that altered climates on Earth, destroying those species unable to adapt and giving an opportunity to others. This justifies to

23

some extent the Christian theological view that the Creator is a *transcendent* power separate from His creation.

But these were crude methods of which the Destructive Creative force grew tired. So it entered the left-hand side of the human brain and sought to use humanity as its instrument of creation and transformation on Earth, an event which occurred in history when mankind learned to handle fire – the great destructive and transformative element – instead of just fearing it like all other animals. In the Old Testament this is described as the moment when Eve and Adam ate the fruit of the Tree of Knowledge.

But human beings, like all species, are still bound to existing equilibria by our powerful instincts: the power of Creation thus had to fight every inch to broaden its power over the human mind, and to alienate humanity from its essentially conservative instinctual drives. The cosmic dialectical struggle thus entered the human mind, which thereby became a microcosm of the Universe, expressed in this old wisdom saying: "If you want to understand the human soul, study the Universe; if you want to understand the Universe, study the human soul."

The Reason for Patriarchal Monotheism

Why would a cosmic force of Creation seek to become humanity's only god and enjoin its worshippers to destroy all forms of Nature worship wherever they had the power to do so? Because this force wanted to use men as its instruments of self-awareness and creativity to transform their living environments according to the plans this force helped them to formulate in their minds. But Nature worship acts as a powerful brake on human willingness to change its natural environments.

You cannot build houses, temples or bridges from wood without cutting down a large number of living trees: this is more difficult when human beings recognise them as living beings, fellow children of the Great Earth Mother inhabited by elemental spirits. You cannot build offices, bridges or railways of iron or steel without spoiling many a landscape to mine the coal and iron ore underneath it. So alienating human beings from their living environment, making them look at all other living beings as "things" and raw materials rather than as brothers and sisters, was an essential prerequisite to making them the industrious servants of the force of Creation.

The Reasons for Constant War

Human beings can become alienated from their living environment through a strong sense of individual and tribal identity centred in their brains behind their eyes. Nothing fosters and strengthens this sense of separate identity more than warfare, when you must kill before you are killed yourself, and you can only do so by being strongly centred in your own body, time and place.

So the God of Creation was also the Eternal Lord of Hosts, and the more monotheistic peoples have also been the most successfully militarily aggressive. Warfare fosters also in all cultures a greater willingness to adapt and to accept new inventions in order to survive, thus contributing to a speeding up of the human technological evolution that the force of Destructive Creation promotes.

Why Women have been Downgraded and Oppressed

It is much more difficult to alienate women from their instinctual feelings since they carry children in their womb for nine months and then nurture them for years until they are strong enough to fend for themselves; nor would it be desirable since offspring do require their mother's love to grow up healthy and strong. But men, whose role in the reproductive process is so much briefer, can be alienated more easily, the more effectively if they are made to look down on women and their subjective feelings. Hence the monotheistic worshippers of the force of Creation are strongly patriarchal and reserve all political activity to men.

The Reason for Sexual Repression

Since Nature has programmed all living beings to be strongly attracted to the opposite sex to reproduce the species and has made sexual unions highly pleasurable, men had to be taught to regard such pleasure as sinful and shameful. Hence the strong anti-erotic bias of Christianity, and the practice of female clitoral mutilation in many African Muslim countries to prevent women from finding any pleasure in sexual intercourse.

I leave to a subsequent book the description of the historical tests that validate this theory.

COSMIC CONSCIOUSNESS

In January 1958 Dayonis – our new HPS since the break with Doreen – and Jack Bracelin told me that since I had been in the coven 12 months and was competent at raising power I could now be raised to the 2nd degree. This ceremony took place again at the Candlemas festival. Unlike my initiation this ceremony did not bring me closer to the Goddess although I found the journey into the underworld very moving.

Two days after my elevation I was returning from a lecture on comparative religion in central London to my caravan. I did not own a car in those days, the last shuttle train had already left Watford and buses ran only as far as Garston Garage after 11 p.m., so I set out to cover the last two miles on foot. It was a clear full moon night with only the odd wisp of cumulus cloud passing across the moon's face like a caress. As I walked along the A405 I contemplated the moon absent-mindedly as I wrestled once more with the problem that had been nagging me in recent weeks.

How could I know that the conceptual structure of Dialectical Pantheism was the right one, and that all the great minds that had contributed to Christian theology over the past two millennia – Paul, Augustine, Thomas Aquinas, Luther, Calvin and many more – had implicitly been wrong? Wasn't this rather childish hubris?

As I looked up at the moon, my mind wandered to a contemplation of the eternal ballet of interlocking circular dances performed by the heavenly bodies: the Moon revolving around the Earth every 29.5 days, the Earth around the Sun every 365.25 days, and – who knows – perhaps the solar system itself around some larger unseen centre of attraction. These revolutions bear a strong resemblance to those performed by the electrons around the nuclei of the atoms in each cell of our bodies, and in all energy and matter.

Could it be that the solar system, and each of the other stars visible to us, are only atoms in a cell of the body of some giant being, in whose life the whole of known cosmic and terrestrial history is but a short breath? Conversely, are whole races and civilisations rising and falling every second on each electron of each atom of my body? Does the Universe fold into itself not just in space, but in such a meeting of the infinitely large with the infinitesimally small?

This speculation seemed to unlock a door of consciousness. Like Cocteau's Orphée, I suddenly walked through the mirror out of space and time. Leaving my body walking along the A405 far behind, my consciousness expanded to encompass the whole sky, and then the whole Universe.

I was the calm placid Moon which I had been contemplating so intently, the fiery furnace of the Sun, the whole Earth and its mountains and valleys, rivers, lakes and seas, and the mighty forces that had moulded it and all the other planets of the solar system, and all the other stars and their planets and satellites. I thrilled to the ecstasy of their dance, and each of their revolutions was like one of my breaths.

Then suddenly the cosmos within my consciousness was filled with all the souls of all the sentient beings that had ever lived and ever would live, and I was every one of them. I was every king and queen, general, priest, artisan and peasant since the dawn of history, as well as every beast, bird and insect of the forest. I was every passionate pair of lovers of every race and animal breed since the beginning of time, and every couple of parents tenderly nurturing their young.

But I was also every lion and tiger chasing a gazelle, and every gazelle being chased. I was full of the terror of villagers overrun by a plundering army, but I also thrilled to the soldiers' excitement in their pillage and raping. I was every Jew starved or gassed to death in a Nazi concentration camp, but also every one of their SS guards. In my head a voice was saying: "There is still a spark of divinity and hope for redemption in the man who has the courage to face the rapes and murders he has committed in past wars, and even the fact that he enjoyed them at the time. But there is little hope for that lowest of creatures: the man who 'was only obeying orders'."

I was the One soul of the Universe, the deepest part of all beings, that has always been and always will be, and survives the death of mortal bodies and their egos and even of the planets on which they live.

The vision began to fade, and far below me I became dimly aware of a pair of feet walking along a country road. Then I remembered the intellectual problem that had been bothering me and began to match every religious myth, belief and dogma that I could think of against the fading vision of universe and eternity. To my shocked surprise, they all fitted!

Christian beliefs that had defied all logical reasoning suddenly appeared easy and self-evident. Had I been an anguished would-be Christian wrestling with intellectual doubts, these would have been washed away and I would have returned from the experience joyfully proclaiming I had "met Christ". But I had long ceased to be a would-be Christian and I continued to match against the fading vision Jewish, Moslem, Hindu, Buddhist, Taoist and old Mediterranean polytheistic beliefs. They all fitted equally well.

The heavenly choirs of the Christian paradise described the ecstasy of unity with the cosmos as well but no better than the Mohammedan paradise in which one is attended by beautiful houris, or the land of rest and recuperation for tired souls on the far shores of the Styx, or the Buddhist nirvana, or the Hindu dance of Shiva.

Desperate for some guidance, I started reciting theological propositions that in terms of human logic are mutually exclusive:

"There is but One God." True.
"There is an infinite number of gods and goddesses struggling
    with and loving each other, and Life as we know it is the fruit
    of their interplay." Equally true.
"There is no God." Just as true.
"Good and Evil are opposite forces, forever struggling for the
    soul of humanity." True.
"Good and Evil both derive from the One, and are equally
    important aspects of the divine scheme of things." True.

By then the vision had faded completely, and I was wholly back in space and time. Looking about me to locate myself, I reckoned I could not have walked more than four paces during the entire experience. Dazed, I continued on my walk home.

For the next three days I seemed to move about my daily routines in a state of moral weightlessness, with all the moral and ethical programming of my childhood wiped out. I had been given complete freedom of choice.

On the positive side I had lost my fear of death and of the destruction of life by a nuclear holocaust. I now knew spiritually and emotionally what until then had only been an intellectual postulate: the essential part of me was immortal and eternal and would survive the death of my physical body and its conscious memories. Death would be but the final curtain on my current role on the stage of life, and the prelude to learning a new one. Even if our asinine governments blew the world up in a nuclear holocaust and thereby brought the higher forms of mammal life to an end, I would still be there among the forces present on the irradiated Earth, helping to initiate a new cycle of evolution.

I had also lost the somewhat élitist fear shared by many university graduates: that of losing my identity in the vast sea of suburban middle class mediocrity in which I commuted every day to and from central London. As I travelled to and from work I looked on my fellow passengers in a new light. Behind each one of those conventional clothes styles and closed expressions was another incarnation of the One soul of the Universe, with his or her own unique set of gifts and handicaps, joys and sorrows, set of friends, lovers, spouse and children, whose experiences might well be a more entertaining act for the One than my own.

This newly found security did not wholly compensate, however, for the terrifying amorality of the One that I had experienced, and the equally frightening freedom of moral choice that it gave me. I felt free to become a social predator, victim, healer or detached observer. I could join the Foreign Legion or a criminal fraternity, or a secret police force holding down an oppressed majority in the interests of a favoured few, or a revolutionary, or a member of a religious order devoting itself to the relief of hunger and suffering, or of an enclosed contemplative order. Or I could lead a conventional middle class life as breadwinner of a nuclear family.

Each role would be equally valid in the light of the experience I had just had, an equal contribution to the infinite diversity of Life that it would thereby affirm, as long as I had freely chosen it for myself and enjoyed it. Boring oneself and thereby the One watcher within was the only sin.

My own choices had in the past been in the direction of idealistic activism: for European federalism in my student days; more recently, seeking the pattern of religious beliefs that would best help human beings pursue knowledge and a rising standard of living in harmony rather than in conflict with each other and with Nature. Seeing these ideals put on a par with those of all the forces of oppression and conflict by the all-encompassing all-seeing but detached One, as just some of many games and roles on the stage of Life, seemed suddenly to rob them of all dignity and meaning. It was my dark night of the soul, that follows so frequently a 2nd degree elevation.

Three days later, I was still as dazed by my experience as I had been immediately afterwards. Then suddenly it was as if a voice spoke in my head to say: "You have had a glimpse of the Infinity beyond Space and the Eternity beyond Time, to which you will return at the end of your physical life. But you cannot go on living on that plane without going mad. You have been incarnated as a time and space bound human being of flesh and blood in a time and space bound material world with a purpose to fulfil, and you must accept the limitations of your condition, including the apparent logical mutual exclusiveness of different aspects of the Eternal reality.

"You cannot, therefore, live by all the aspects of Infinity and Eternity at once, but must choose which partial aspect you will live by.

Choose carefully, because while some aspects of the Eternal reality can help you live a fuller, more effective and happier life, others could destroy you and the world in which you live. Trust your own inner sense of Truth to guide you: the aspects of the Infinite reality that can help you will appear to you spontaneously as "true", while you will be instinctively repelled by those dogmas, beliefs and ways of life that are destructive of your integrity, health and those of the world in which you live.

"In thus choosing the mental constructs and myths most suitable to your age, do not be so arrogant, however, as to proclaim them "truer" on the plane of Eternity than other beliefs chosen by other men living in other times or cultures than your own. If they chose differently from you, it was not necessarily their inner sense of Truth that was deficient, just the circumstances of the age in which they lived which called for a different response."

The inner voice gave me a huge sense of relief. I did not have to prove Paul, Augustine, Thomas Aquinas *et al* deluded to validate my own Pantheist cosmology and Wiccan practice. Their ages were indeed vastly different from my own, and may well have required a different religious response. And the theory of Dialectical Pantheism explained the Christian Church's intolerance and cruelty to different believers at the height of its power.

HOW SPELLS WORK

As a rational speculative person I naturally wondered how spells worked. Given that we were raising power by running around fast, I imagined it was a case of us raising extra energy and then transmitting it telepathically to the person we were trying to heal, thereby increasing his or her energy to enable him or her to recover faster from her/his illness. But two spells soon convinced me that it is a great deal more complicated than this, and that other forces are frequently involved.

SAVING THE CLUB

Gerald Gardner had bought the few acres of Hertfordshire woodland in 1945, on which the Fiveacres nudist club was developed, to be the cover for the witchcraft coven he would form with the initiates who wrote to him. But he had no interest in running the club itself, and appointed a salaried administrator to run the club on his behalf.

This man deliberately ran the club at a loss by setting unrealistically high requirements for membership, hoping thereby to persuade Gerald eventually to sell the club to him at a low price. By 1956 Fiveacres had only 40 members. But Gerald saw through the ploy, sacked the administrator and appointed his right-hand man in the coven, Jack Bracelin, in his place. This time he did not pay a salary, but told Jack he could live off the club's income.

The sacked administrator had not finished with us, however. He was a friend of Ernest Stanley, the puritanical owner of the North Kent naturist club and leading light in the Central Council of British Naturism (CCBN). He persuaded Stanley that under Jack's management our club was becoming a hotbed of witchcraft and loose living, and should be refused admission to the CCBN as well as advertising space in *Health and Efficiency*, the leading naturist monthly magazine. With all advertising refused to him, Jack got only a few new members in his first year of management and found it impossible to live off the club. In January 1958 at the end of his tether, he asked us to work a spell to ensure a lifting of the advertising embargo.

Events now took a strange turn. A year earlier the Danish naturist magazine *Sun & Health* had run a forum on sexual education for naturists' children. I contributed an article recommending linking sex with love in the minds of adolescents, but saying we should be consistent. When teenagers fell in love, they should be allowed to give their love a sexual expression subject of course to the usual contraceptive precautions. Although I had written it as far back as July 1957, *Sun & Health* published it in their January 1958 issue.

This touched all of Ernest Stanley's most sensitive inhibitions. In the February 1958 issue of *Health & Efficiency* he published a libellous article accusing me of encouraging adult sexual abuse of children, and naming our club as a front for "witchcraft and black magic". Jack had a lawyer friend who promptly slapped an injunction on W. H. Smith and all magazine distributors to stop distributing the magazine on pain of being joined in the forthcoming libel suit. A day later, the offending issue disappeared from all newsagents' shelves.

Three weeks later, Jack received a letter from a firm of publishers informing him they had bought *Health & Efficiency* from the previous owners and had put a new editorial team in charge. They offered him three months' free advertising for his club, and normal commercial terms thereafter, if he would please lift the injunction on the magazine's distributors. The club was saved.

HEALING FRANÇOISE

In October 1958 I spent a week's vacation at the Brussels World Exhibition. On the last day, I sat opposite a pretty Belgian girl at lunch and we spent the afternoon touring the exhibition together. She informed me that she was epileptic and had had an especially severe attack four years earlier, when she was 18. This had deprived her of her intellectual memory and she was unable to take any abstract or technical information in, but she didn't care: she was frozen in a state of superficial contentment. I commiserated and we parted after exchanging addresses.

It was only in the train back to London that it occurred to me that as an initiated witch I should be able to help Françoise with my coven's aid. So I wrote to her guardedly saying that my friends and I conducted experiments in spiritual healing. We were not very good at it, so could promise her nothing, except that at the worst it would make her no worse. If she was willing to cooperate, we would do what we could do for her. She should just send us a photograph and a lock of hair, pray to the Virgin Mary (as she was Catholic), and send us reports on her progress.

Our first working for Françoise took place on Saturday 1 November, when the full moon coincided with Halloween. Françoise's next letter reported that her intellectual memory was returning and her emotions had unfrozen: she was very depressed and spent hours weeping uncontrollably. She had frequent minor epileptic fits in which she fell down and promptly picked herself up again.

So we tried again at the next Full Moon meeting on 29 November. A week later our High Priestess Dayonis, Jack Bracelin and I were visiting our anaesthetist member and his wife at their home in Winchester when we decided to do an impromptu Wiccan meeting. Whom to work for? Why, Françoise of course, with me once again as the energy transmitter. This time I heard irritated voices in my head saying: "Stop bugging us! Your request for Françoise has been received and understood: now leave the rest to us. You can do no more." When I got up, I told them what had happened and that we would not be working for Françoise any more.

In her next letter, Françoise reported an astonishing influx of energy. She had signed up for two university courses in the New Year and was going out dancing every night. Then nothing for nearly six months.

At Whitsun 1959 I was due to attend the College of Europe Alumni Association's weekend in Bruges. So I wrote to Françoise on the off chance asking how she was, and whether I might visit her on the way. An enthusiastic reply came by return of post inviting me for the weekend and saying she and her mother would meet me off the boat at Ostend. As I approached the car, her mother said she was so happy to meet the man who had healed Françoise.

"Healed? When?"

"Why, after my accident" replied Françoise.

"What accident?"

"Oh! I suppose you don't know since I haven't written to you. On 24 January, I was being driven home from a ball by an escort who had had too much to drink. We had a head-on crash in which I was flung through the windscreen. I was in coma for five days and needed 13 stitches to my scalp (she showed me the scars of some), but when I came to, I was cured of epilepsy. I haven't had a fit since then."

On returning to London I checked with our anaesthetist member, who confirmed that epilepsy is a symptom of a faulty circuit in the brain, which can often be cured by a sudden traumatic shock. Unfortunately, the effects are wholly random (my friend could easily have been killed or crippled by her accident) so that it is not possible to base a therapy on this knowledge. Unfortunately, I then lost touch with Françoise so don't know whether the cure held. She was beginning to fall in love with me, and I had to either marry her or break off the relationship.

I participated in many more remarkable healing and fate alteration spells in those early years. I have described them in my earlier book *Religion without Beliefs* and will do so again in a forthcoming book about spellcasting techniques.

AN EXPERIENCE OF BLACK MAGIC

Our spell of January 1958 had lifted the advertising embargo on Fiveacres and members now came flooding in. But Jack Bracelin needed to secure his future for the time after Gerald's death. His lawyer friend advised him to found a private company, Ancient Crafts Ltd, into which ownership of the club would be vested. All shares in the company would be jointly held by Gerald Gardner and Jack: in that way on Gerald's death the company and the club would automatically become Jack's property alone.

It appears that Gerald's long time friend Arnold Crowther warned Gerald against this arrangement, because at one coven meeting Jack, looking tense, told us that Arnold was bothering Gerald, and that Gerald had asked us to do a binding on Arnold. This was almost certainly a lie: Gerald had no reason to wish to bind his friend Arnold: the initiative must have come from Jack himself.

As I was such an effective power channel for the coven, Jack asked me to be the transmitter of the binding to Arnold. In later years I would never have agreed to such a request, but I was inexperienced and eager to make myself useful. So I knelt in front of the altar and focused on Arnold's picture while the rest of the coven started moving widdershins around the circle.

Suddenly without losing consciousness I lost control of my body, and was made to cackle with a fiendish laugh while belabouring the altar with my athame. Fortunately, we had an experienced Kabbalist named Omar in our coven. Realising what was happening he placed himself behind me, put his hands above my head and declaimed: "In nomine Patri, Filii et Spiritu Sanctu..." Whatever had possessed me fled the circle immediately and I regained control of my body. "That was a Catholic formula you used then", I said with surprise, "are you Catholic?" "No," replied Omar, "I have just found it a very effective banishing spell."

That ended the binding spell on Arnold Crowther, who probably didn't feel anything at all. I have never since then participated in any binding spell nor any other form of black magic on anybody, and would never do so in the future.

A TRADITIONAL WITCH

One of the new coven members who had written to Gerald and been passed on to Jack and Dayonis was a Norfolk squire's wife, owner of a pack of hunting beagles, who led the local hunt with her husband, as well as a traditional witches' coven that was its inner core. She had come to check us out, and circled with us for several months.

When asked how her coven cast spells she replied that they all sat in a circle on chairs and just visualised the desired result. But she had no trouble working with our methods. When we raised cones of power by dancing in a circle, she used to run around at great speed with great whoops of joy. She contributed a lot of joy and power to our circle, but withdrew from it after the unwelcome publicity caused by Charles Cardell's machinations.

Her brief membership of our coven confirmed that there were other witchcraft traditions in England other than Gardner's, and that magical power comes from our focused thoughts alone. Everything else – ritual nudity, running around, or simply sitting quietly and meditating – are just techniques for putting us into an altered state of consciousness.

THE FIRST WITCH WAR

In 1958 Charles Cardell, a rich psychotherapist with a flat in Chelsea, set out to discredit Gerald Gardner with a view to taking over the nascent Goddess worshipping current. He induced one of his patients, an unstable woman called Olive Green, to write to Gerald and ask him to train her. Gerald didn't refer her to Dayonis and Jack – or perhaps they had turned her down – so Gerald undertook all her training himself, of which she passed the details on to Cardell. After six months she terminated the training and wrote an extremely wounding letter to Gerald calling him a fraud and a pervert.

Cardell now contacted journalists at the *Sunday Chronicle* (the ancestor of today's *Sunday Mirror*) suggesting they do an exposé of our coven. On a date when according to the Book of Shadows there should have been a meeting at the Bricket Wood witches' cottage, Cardell, a reporter and a photographer climbed over the Fiveacres fence and approached the cottage. It was empty and nothing was happening there, probably because it was a weekday night and we would have done our Full Moon working or seasonal Sabbath the previous Saturday.

The reporter and photographer now visited Gerald in his Holland Park flat and bullyingly accused him of deceiving the public in his interviews by claiming to have a coven with members that didn't exist. To defend himself Gerald weakly named a few coven members, including our anaesthetist member. After they had left, Gerald realised he had broken his oath of secrecy, had a severe attack of asthma and fled to Jersey, leaving Jack to clear up the mess.

Jack immediately instructed all coven members to refuse to talk to the reporters, thereby refusing them the corroboration they required. But the reporters inveigled one of our woman members into talking, saying it would be better for her if they printed just what she had told them instead of them engaging in more lurid speculations. They now had the corroboration of Gerald's names that they needed.

It could have been serious for our anaesthetist member's professional career if his name had been published, so Jack took an emergency measure. To kill the *Sunday Chronicle* story he offered an exposé to its rival Sunday paper the *People* naming all those coven members who volunteered, including Dayonis, Jack, another woman member and myself, because we felt less vulnerable. The *People*'s story came out the Sunday before the one on which the *Sunday Chronicle* were planning to run their story, which made the latter's used goods which they had to kill. No one at *The Economist Intelligence Unit* read the *People*, so I wasn't even given a friendly ribbing about it.

Cardell now invited Dayonis, Jack and me to his Chelsea flat to listen to a tape recording of him talking to the *Sunday Chronicle* reporter pleading with him to leave us alone. He then told us: "This is what happens when you associate with a shameless self-publicist like Gardner. Why don't you join my group, which has true esoteric knowledge and is really secret so you wouldn't be bothered by the press in the future?" But he didn't inspire us with any confidence, and we weren't going to join a man who had instigated this mess, nor abandon Gerald for whom we all had a great deal of affection for all his faults.

We later heard via the rumour mill that Cardell had a group of initiates who met in the South Downs, but they soon disappeared without trace. Cardell's last blast were the Rex Nemorensis (his magical name) papers attacking Gerald published in an American journal in 1964. Cardell was on a power trip whereas Gerald was disinterestedly trying to serve the Goddess. The Gardnerian tradition was contacted, Cardell's was not.

This experience with the popular press made us very shy of any sort of publicity thereafter. In order to be left alone, Jack launched a rumour that the coven had broken up in the wake of the *People* exposé. This explains why after Gerald's death it was Eleanor Bone and Patricia Crowther who carried the torch of publicity for Gardnerian witchcraft, and not the older Bricket Wood coven.

JACK BRACELIN

In 1959 I met my companion Gillian into whose flat I moved in September 1959. We married in August 1960 and Jack Bracelin organised a great party for us at Fiveacres, at which Lois Bourne, who had become High Priestess after Dayonis left for Canada in October 1959, blessed our union in the Goddess' name.

In 1960 I started working for a computer manufacturer, who moved Gillian and me to the Manchester area in October 1961. From then on we circled only with the Bricket Wood coven intermittently until our return to London in August 1964 shortly after Gerald's death on a cruise ship off the Tunisian coast. By then we had acquired two children and became more family centred as young couples are wont to do.

We arrived back to London in time to witness Jack Bracelin's resignation as coven High Priest and from the coven itself. This left a bad taste in the mouth of many coven members, who thought that Jack had only been interested all along in inheriting the club's ownership.

This is doing the man an injustice. He had been devoted to Gerald who was a father figure to him, and had worked tirelessly for over seven years to defend the coven from the scrapes in which Gerald's taste for publicity could and on one occasion had landed it. His friendship with Idries Shah showed also that he was genuinely interested in self-development and esoteric knowledge.

But after Gerald's death he asked himself whether the Book of Shadows' simplified ceremonial magic rituals expressed his own religious feelings, and concluded they did not. Membership of a secretive coven that was not growing the Craft in numbers must also have seemed a dead end to him. In 1966 he married a young woman in a Catholic church ceremony, which the Bricket Wood coven regarded as a further betrayal.

He had not, however, lost interest in promoting life-affirming Goddess values, and thought that the flower-child period of the late 1960s represented its true expression. In order to help promote it he mortgaged the club to raise the capital to found a discotheque with strobe light effects in London's West End. It was a financial disaster, and from then on he was always in debt.

He remained faithful to Gerald, however, in that he allowed the coven to continue holding its meetings at the witches' cottage, and provided cover for it by organising club parties on the weekends preceding major festivals so as to deflect possible curiosity from our own celebrations in the cottage. We had, however, to pay rent on the plot on which the cottage and a neighbouring hut stood, for which the non-nudist coven members were reluctant to pay their share. In 1972 we started meeting at our new High Priestess' and High Priest's house in North London in the winter months, using the cottage only in spring, summer and early autumn.

Finally in 1975 we received a demand to help pay for the club's electrification, at which we decided to stop using the cottage altogether and sell its plot to another club member. This transaction closed in March 1976. Three months later his creditors closed in on Jack and he lost ownership of the club, which since then has had no association with Wicca except historical. Paid a small pension by the new owner of Fiveacres, Jack retired to Greece where he died of a heart attack in 1983.

4

AN EVENING WITH ALEX SANDERS

In October 1965 my wife and I were off again, when I was posted to Prague as leader of a technical support group for English Electric computers sold to the Czech Railways and a steelworks in Ostrava. My wife returned in September 1966 after we had discovered that our three year old daughter was deaf, and I followed in April 1967. When I returned London was in its swinging phase during the flower-child period, and their paper was a weekly called the *International Times*.

In 1968 one of the IT issues carried a letter from one Alex Sanders. He wrote that he was a witch from a religion fully in tune with flower-child values, that he had recently moved down from Manchester and would welcome visits from people in the scene to his flat near Notting Hill. Keen to broaden our range of acquaintances in the witchcraft scene I wrote to him saying my wife and I were Gardnerian craft initiates belonging to a coven, therefore not candidates to join his coven, but would welcome an opportunity to meet him socially.

A few days later we got a telephone call from one of his acolytes asking whether we were associated with Rae Bone. "No," I replied, "I know Rae Bone but we are not members of her coven." A couple more days elapsed and we were invited to meet the Sanders one Friday evening at 8 p.m.

When we arrived on the due date, we were met by Alex, three other coven members and Maxine – pregnant and radiating Goddess energy – sitting quietly in a corner. She was so beautiful I would have gladly joined their coven for her sake. Hardly had we been introduced and offered seats that he launched into an hour long monologue explaining Craft theology – in which he was sound – but mainly describing his career in the Craft which was in the wilder ranges of fantasy. He described at various times three different versions of how he had come into the Craft, including the story of his initiation by his grandmother at the age of six on the kitchen floor.

He described an open air ritual he and his coven had performed on Alderley Edge in 1963 – a hill park near Manchester – which had been watched by "30 000 people". Maxine and the other initiates wriggled uncomfortably: "Perhaps not quite as many, Alex!" they said.

It so happens that at the time my wife and I had been living in Altrincham near Manchester, and one of my colleagues said to me in the office: "I hear there were some witches on Alderley Edge last night." So the ritual had taken place but was not mentioned in the papers. It had probably been watched by 30 people who had passed by walking their dogs, but not 30 000! How would so many have known about it in the absence of prior publicity, and would Alderley Edge even hold so many people?

After an hour's non-stop monologue, Alex was out of breath and needed a cup of tea, but wasted no time in putting on a tape recording of *himself* reciting the *Charge of the Goddess* in his flat Mancunian accent. At this point I should have stopped him and said: "Stop! Take that tape off immediately! I first heard The Charge at my initiation and on special occasions since then recited by the High Priestess. I don't want to hear it recited by a man outside the circle!"

If I had he would have realised that we were genuine Craft initiates and we might then have had an intelligent conversation. Because I realised later that his behaviour, notably not checking us out when we first arrived, meant that he thought we were undercover press reporters pretending to be initiates. He did not know of the Bricket Wood coven and thought Rae Bone's were the only Gardnerian covens in the London area: since we had disclaimed being her members, we couldn't be genuine Gardnerians.

But I didn't unfortunately, out of misplaced politeness. And so by the time the tape had finished Alex had also finished his cup of tea and launched into another hour's monologue. I managed to get a question in, commenting on the similarity of his rituals with those of the Gardnerian Book of Shadows. He acknowledged this but maintained Gerald had got them from him, and that he had been practising the Craft long before Gerald. Since he thought we were no witches, he didn't know that we knew the Book of Shadows rituals we practised had been put together by Gerald and Doreen Valiente. Especially the Charge of the Goddess, which she had written using a modified front end from Leland's *Aradia, Gospel of the Witches* and a back end that reads like Crowley.

In the last half-hour of his second monologue Alex talked about his experiences of ritual magic. His voice became sadder and less self-assured as he said: "I once spent a week doing the Abra-Melin ritual" (to achieve the "knowledge and conversation of the holy guardian angel" in Aleister Crowley's sonorous words) "but I was probably insufficiently purified beforehand, because I nearly went mad!" You can cut out the "nearly" I thought to myself.

It was 10 p.m. when he finally stopped talking and said: "Now let's hear about you". But my wife jumped up and said: "I am sorry but we have to go because we have a baby sitter deadline!" which was true, but we could probably have stayed another half-hour. As we climbed into our car my wife hissed: "I never want to meet that man again! He is full of power and doesn't know what to do with it: such people are dangerous!"

Whatever liberties Gerald had taken with the factual truth Alex trumped him in spades, but I concluded that he was not a calculating but a compulsive liar: he really appeared to believe the mutually incompatible stories of how he entered the Craft at the time that he told them, and probably also the 30 000 watchers of his Alderley Edge ritual. Coming from a humbler background than Gerald's rich merchant family he probably needed his fantasies to bolster a vulnerable ego. His long years of solitary Kabbalistic magic may also have made him lose the sense of discrimination between what happens on the astral or etheric planes and what happens in mundane reality.

THE ALEXANDRIAN CRAFT

It wasn't just in his fantasies that Alex trumped Gerald. Gerald had produced 30 "Laws of the Craft" out of his hat, mainly to get his way in political arguments like the one that preceded the split with Doreen. Alex added 130 more laws of his own devising for a total of 160 and apparently over 100 more for the second degree.

Gerald had borrowed his initiation and circle opening rituals from Freemasonry and the Greater Key of Solomon to provide some atmosphere. Alex introduced Kabbalistic rituals wholesale into his version of Wicca, including pathworkings on the Tree of Life, and the recitation of the Lesser Banishing Ritual of the Pentagram during circle opening. Having thus turned his covens into magical lodges, he did the same as all adepts of the Western Mysteries: he introduced an intensive system of initiatory training to ensure his initiates accepted his version of the Craft and his magical techniques.

Like all magical lodges Alexandrian covens are also much more hierarchical and authoritarian than Gardnerian ones. Their high priestess and high priest together decide alone on which postulants to initiate into their covens, whereas admission to Gardnerian covens is by consensus of all existing members.

The well known Wiccan author Vivianne Crowley was initiated into Maxine's coven in 1973 and later received a Gardnerian cross-initiation into the Whitecroft line. Asked about the differences between the two traditions at a conference in 1990 she replied: "Alexandrians are much better trained, but Gardnerians do far more spiritual healing and seem to have more fun!"

Since Alex Sanders' death in 1988 Vivianne has striven to converge the two traditions, at least in Britain. Many formally Gardnerian covens now also engage in pre-initiation training, while many formally Alexandrian covens have cut down on the Kabbalistic elements in their rituals, notably dropping the Lesser Banishing Ritual of the Pentagram. And both traditions treat their respective "Laws" with the disregard they deserve.

PUBLICITY

In the early 1970s Alex also trumped Gerald in his publicity methods. Whereas Gerald was just too keen to give interviews even to the red top press, Alex and Maxine got into the newspapers in 1972 by performing a phoney Black Mass on stage to an audience of businessmen in a Bournemouth night club. Alex also had a Craft initiation ceremony (not of a real person) videotaped, which he then sold widely. On that tape Alex as the High Priest is robed whereas all the other coven members are nude, thus distancing himself from them.

These actions, as well as the publication of books with emetic titles like *King of the Witches* did not endear him to Gardnerian initiates, which accounts for the mutual antipathy between the Gardnerian and Alexandrian traditions of Wicca until his death in 1988. But for all his lurid publicity he did more good to the Craft than harm by bringing it to many more good people in the 1970s than if they had had to satisfy Gardnerian covens' much more demanding requirements. A 1970s joke on the differences between Gardnerian and Alexandrian Wicca went like this: "To become a Gardnerian you have first to find a coven – no easy task because of their secrecy – then meet them socially for around ten years, and then if you are lucky you might be offered a place in their coven when a vacancy occurs. But to become an Alexandrian you just have to walk slowly past Alex's front door!"

In 1973 Alex and Maxine separated and the publicity stunts ceased abruptly. Maxine continued to run a training coven from her flat in Notting Hill until recently, but Alex retired to a house in Sussex, where he gave private instructions to a select group of disciples until he died of cancer at Beltane in 1988.

ROOTS OF WICCAN INDIVIDUALISM

I have often wondered why the Goddess chose two such flawed characters as Gerald Gardner and Alex Sanders to bring Her worship and spell-casting knowledge back to the West, instead of more credible and charismatic teachers such as Idries Shah. I came to the conclusion that it was intentional to force Wiccans to think for themselves from the beginning because it was impossible to turn either Gerald or Alex into a guru. If I had met Idries before Gerald I would probably have sat at his feet for ten years or until he kicked me out and said: "Fred, you're on your own now!"

Compare Wiccan individualism with the topdown hierarchical authority of Western Mysteries lodges, or Indian guru-led movements like the Rajneeshis or the Hare Krishnas. The Rajneeshi movement has shrunk since Rajneesh's death in 1991, and his remaining followers sell tapes of his admittedly very witty philosophical lectures. ISKCON members can only dance around the streets in yellow or orange robes chanting "Hare Krishna, Hare Krishna, Krishna Krishna, Hare Hare!" and sell or give away Swami Pramupada's commented edition of the Bhagavad Gita. Even OTO publications of the 1970s and 1980s confined themselves to reprinting Crowley articles from the *Equinox*.

But Wicca continues to expand since Alex Sanders' death, and attempts by some to fill his shoes and become a new "king of the witches" have been met with scorn.

MAXINE

I never met Alex Sanders again, but 22 years later at a garden party preceding the first annual conference of the Fellowship of Isis in 1990 I saw a blonde woman wave to me from a distance. Later she approached me in the bar and said: "Hi! I am Maxine Sanders. We have met before but I can't remember when, so tell me!" I related the story of my visit to their flat in 1968 and she smiled as she said: "That sounds like Alex!"

I have met Maxine on a few occasions since then and found her to be a powerful witch who doesn't need to embroider the truth. The training she gives her initiates is said to be rigorous and she speaks her mind with no concessions to political correctness.

5

ENCOUNTERS WITH ELEMENTALS AND MY GUARDIAN GODDESS

THE IRISH WITCH

In August 1969 my wife Gillian had to go into University College Hospital for 48 hours for a minor operation. In the women's ward was a small Irish woman some of whose turns of phrases rang bells with Gillian. On the second day all the other women were discharged so that Gillian and the Irish woman had the ward to themselves for a few hours before the fresh intake arrived.

Sitting on the Irish woman's bed Gillian asked her: "You're a witch, aren't you? Don't be afraid, I'm one too!". The Irish woman then told Gillian her grandmother had told her: "If you are ever in trouble or need something badly enough, go into your bedroom, lock the door, take all your clothes off and call on the Little People!" Neither her husband, a builder's labourer, nor any of their seven children knew of her magical knowledge: they were a strongly Catholic family and all went to Mass every Sunday.

This experience proved that ritual nudity for magical effectiveness was no invention of Gerald's but has a long pedigree. It also showed that witchcraft and magic are religiously neutral and not necessarily non-Christian.

A LESSON

For the first 13 years after my initiation I was very much a circle witch just as some people are Sunday Christians. My wife and I were happy to circle with our friends in the Bricket Wood coven when we were in

London, but thought little about the Craft between coven meetings or when we were living abroad.

In 1970 I accepted the position of European Editor of the Auerbach Computer Technology Reports and moved to the Philadelphia area to learn about the Auerbach style and editing methods. Suddenly everything started to go wrong. I soon discovered that I was heavily overqualified to be an Auerbach editor, with colleagues straight out of university who were all about 10 to 15 years younger than myself, who already had 10 years' experience of the computer industry. I did, however, learn to write clearly and concisely, which stood me in good stead in writing articles and books in later years.

Shortly after our arrival in the Philadelphia area we read an article about witches' covens in the local paper. I wrote the coven a letter c/o the paper telling them we were initiated witches from England looking for a local coven. But I got only a humorous reply asking me to show evidence that my wife shed no tears.

My then 7 year old daughter Helen was deaf but had been taught by my wife to lip read and to express herself in a normal voice. We had been able to keep her in normal schools with small classes until then, and a school in New Jersey promised to teach her in the same way, on the basis of which promise we rented an apartment near the same school. But at the beginning of the autumn term her class teacher refused to teach her after she had got up to go to the toilet without asking permission, and the principal gave in to the teacher.

To cap it all my wife fell ill with an acute urinary infection and had to go into hospital just as she was about to start a teaching job in a local private school and she lost that opportunity.

As James Bond said: "Once is happenstance, twice could be a coincidence, but three times must be enemy action!" Some power was trying to tell me something, so I asked earnestly on an evening walk: "Why is so much going wrong at the same time?" The following night I had a dream in which a voice told me: "It's because you are not practising your religion!" I began immediately to cast a protective circle around our apartment every evening before going to bed, and slowly my wife's health and my opportunities at Auerbach began to improve.

In April 1971 we returned to England and bought a house in Chorleywood in Hertfordshire. Although we could again circle with our friends in the Bricket Wood coven I did not give up my practice of drawing a circle around the house every night. Then I explored Chorleywood Common until I found a tree in the nearby wood which spoke to me. Thereafter I walked to that tree every evening after dark

46

and the last dogwalkers had returned home, drew a circle around it and called on the Goddess to protect the health and happiness of my wife, each of our two children by name and myself. I did the same in a nearby wood after we moved to St Albans in 1976, and on Hampstead Heath after we moved to the Hampstead Garden Suburb in 1978.

THE FRIGHTENED ELEMENTALS

For the first few years I used no magical tools but cast the circle with the upraised index and second fingers of my right hand. When I started doing this out of doors around my special tree, I did not use the pompous "I summon, stir and call ye up..." command from the Book of Shadows, but said: "Gentle spirits of Air/Fire/Water/Earth, guardians of the portals of E/S/W/N, please admit me to your realms, join me and guard my circle!"

I soon felt the local elemental spirits taking an interest. I never saw any of them but felt a very faint whispering similar to the noise made by crickets in the Mediterranean but much much fainter. Whenever I called upon the spirits of Air to guard the East (and later West) end of my circle a short gust of wind into my face told me that they were there. Fortunately the spirits of water did not feel it necessary to confirm their presence by making it rain, nor the spirits of fire by causing a forest fire.

I had been working like this for some years when one day I thought: "I must really do things properly" and brought my athame with me the following evening. But no sooner had I brandished this that I felt the elemental spirits around me recoil in horror and within a second they had fled, leaving me alone with my tree feeling an absolute idiot. I never took my athame again with me for my evening circles and slowly the elemental spirits returned to keep me company.

Later I read that elemental spirits do indeed fear all tools made of iron or steel, and no wonder! Aren't such tools used mainly to cut and hurt the trees and other plants that they inhabit? I now recalled the words in my initiation when the wand was presented: "This is the weapon used to summon those spirits for which it would not be meet to use the athame!" Those spirits are all the elemental spirits of the great outdoors. All knives and swords should thus be left at home when casting circles out of doors.

Traditional country wise women and cunning men probably spend most of their spellcasting time out of doors rather than indoors, and working with the local elemental spirits. Gerald thus got it wrong when he wrote into the initiation that "the athame is the true witch's weapon". That is because he had no feeling for elemental spirits: "They are mischievous and best left alone!" he wrote or said on one occasion.

The only time a country wise woman would use her athame out of doors would be to cut medicinal herbs, and then only after asking the plant's permission. The true witch's tool (not weapon) is thus the wand, assuming she or he needs any tools apart from the upraised two fingers.

A PROHIBITION AGAINST CEREMONIAL MAGIC

At the annual Quest conference in January 1975 we heard a lecture from Alan Adams, who taught computing science at the University of East Anglia in Norwich but was also a trained Kabbalist from the Society of Western Mythologists, an offshoot of Dion Fortune's Society of the Inner Light. After describing his magical system in general terms he said he had been asked to found a new lodge in London, which he would guide from afar once it was well established. Anyone interested should leave his address with him and he would inform us of the place, date and time of the introductory lectures when they occurred. Eager to learn new techniques the Bricket Wood high priest, another coven member, and I signed up.

The first introductory lecture was scheduled for the one day in February that I could not possibly attend. I was also active in the local Chorleywood Liberal Party at the time and edited its news-sheet. Impatient and bored with the endless round of fund raising jumble sales, I had published in the news-sheet an open invitation to readers to come to my house on a date in February to discuss Liberal Party policy issues: that was precisely the date Alan Adams chose for his first introductory lecture. Since I did not know who intended to come I could not phone them up to postpone the political discussion to a later date: in the event one person came.

The second introductory lecture was scheduled in April at a time when I was due to attend the Hannover Fair to gather information on German computers for my consultancy work, so I could not attend that lecture either.

The third lecture was scheduled for a date in May when there were no family obstacles of any sort. My children were both at their respective boarding schools, and my wife had moved to her mother in town during the final examinations of her training course to be a qualified Teacher of the Deaf. I had the house and the calendar entirely to myself.

As we did not own a washing machine at the time I took the laundry down to the local launderette. When I collected it around 5 p.m. and had just paid, something occurred that had never happened before nor since. As I walked towards the glass door I blanked out and walked straight through it without opening it. I came to amid a shower of broken glass, one shard making a deep gash into my left knee. I rushed over to the pharmacy across the road, who applied a temporary bandage and told me to drive myself straight to Accident and Emergency at the nearby Amersham hospital.

I realised then that my guardian spirits were trying to prevent me from attending Alan Adams' introductory lectures, and addressed them: "Your message has been received and understood: you don't want me to attend these lectures. But I shall make that decision consciously myself." So having been stitched and bandaged I nonetheless drove into town for the third introductory lecture.

A Patriarchal Conceptual Framework

Reading the notes of the first two lectures that I had missed I soon realised that Alan's conceptual framework was totally different from mine. He talked about a huge energy called the *Logos* (the Greek word for "concept" translated in the New Testament as "the Word") with which we tiny sparks of individual energy could cooperate if we wanted to help in fulfilling the Logos' plans for the world and humanity. I recognised in this the force of Destructive Creation as described in the theory of Dialectical Pantheism in Chapter 3.

But there was no mention of the balancing Greek concept of *Eros* (the power of Love that should balance the energy of Destructive Creation) so that Adams' framework was as lopsidedly unbalanced and patriarchal as Protestant Christian church theology. Indeed at one point he said that the worst thing that can happen to an initiate of his mysteries is to fall in love. I nonetheless attended also the final two lectures of the series.

In his fifth lecture Alan Adams said his autumn continuation lectures would be reserved to those committing themselves to join the new lodge called The London Group. I hesitated. Although I did not agree with Alan's concepts I thought that if I joined his group nonetheless I might learn some useful magical techniques that I could apply within a

Goddess worshipping Craft context. I was pondering this question during a Liberal Party garden party when voices shouted in my head: "NO!!!" That was it.

This prohibition from the inner planes of having anything to do with ceremonial magic applied to me alone. By inborn temperament I tend to be over-intellectual and need an emotional earthbound mystery cult like Wicca to achieve balance in my spiritual life. Kabbalistic magic would have unbalanced me again by appealing precisely to my already too dominant intellect.

But while the higher powers were thus blocking my path to Kabbalism they laid down a red carpet for our coven high priest. A brilliant mind from a working class background, he had left school at 15 but had taught himself an extensive knowledge of English literature and poetry. He had also learned a great deal of esoteric knowledge in the Junior Branch of the Theosophical Society. Alan Adams was so keen to have him in the London Group that he withdrew his original ban on being a simultaneous member of another occult group, and the group found premises less than ten minutes from where our high priest lived in North London.

Membership of the London Group gave him more intellectual self-confidence and released in him unparalleled magical creativity. In October 1975 he and his companion, our high priestess, put on a magnificent performance of Crowley's Gnostic Mass on Crowley's 100th birthday, which gave them such a power boost that they have since repeated it almost every quarter.

My experience is, however, a warning that not all magical systems are necessarily compatible with each other. Magic is a spiritual technique that is religiously neutral: there are strongly Christian magicians like the Kabbalist Gareth Knight, while Alan Adams concepts were, if not Christian, very left-hand side of the brain oriented.

Meanwhile unconscious inner plane guidance away from Kabbalistic magic has persisted. 15 years later in 1990 I was on a visit in Southern California when one of my local friends asked whether I had anything planned for the following Saturday. "If you don't have anything else to do, why don't you drop in." But on the day itself a group of Wiccans were planning a Pagan ritual for teenagers, and I was curious enough to attend it even though I had not previously thought much on the matter. When I later visited the aforementioned friend he told me he had planned a surprise for me on that evening: an initiation into his *Ordo Templis Astartis*, a Goddess oriented Kabbalistic order, but now it was too late.

UNEXPECTED GUARDIAN DEITIES

For the past 25 years I have prayed to or invoked various goddesses at cross-road trees in woods near my home most evenings. The name "Goddess" appearing to me too impersonal, I experimented with various Greek and Egyptian goddess names in my invocations. Isis produced the greatest resonance of them all, but it still wasn't the perfect fit.

In 1980, I spent a week in Abidjan, capital of the Ivory Coast, as a lecturer in a seminar on computers. On the first day, I visited one of the native markets but found little to interest me. I had left the market and was returning to the hotel when an excited local man caught up with me and showed me a beautiful dark balsawood mask of a goddess figure with white cowrie shells and blue glass beads on her face suggesting a connection with both the sea and the moon. He wanted £60 in local currency for it, which it was well worth, but I had only £15 in cash on me, and he finally let me have it for that amount.

I had not discussed religion with any of the market merchants, so my contact had no rational way of knowing that I was a Goddess worshipper. But it was as if the mask itself had decided to enter my life and had informed its owner (or thief) of this. I took it home with me to England, hung it in my sitting room where it has exuded calm and serenity ever since.

Three years later I bought Migenes Gonzales Wippler's book *Santeria*. It taught me that the name of the Yoruba sea and moon goddess is *Yemaya*. When I next prayed to the Goddess in the evening at my accustomed tree, I tried the name Yemaya. The resonance was immediate, much more powerful than any of the Greek or Egyptian names I had tried until then, stronger even than Isis. I had found my guardian goddess.

In the meantime, I had embarked on a freelance lecturing career on computers and needed an agent to organise bookings and collect fees for me. A small Swiss company named ANUBIT appealed to me because of the closeness of its name to the Egyptian god Anubis. So I employed them, and my fortunes improved immediately, turning the past 20 years into the most successful and prosperous of my whole career. Nor is this the only way in which Anubis has helped me. I often mislay either my purse or my keys around the house. When I have looked five times at all the most obvious spots, I call on Anubis to help me and within a minute I normally find what I am looking for.

Ten years ago, I was browsing in a Paris bookshop and found sets of astrological cards they were selling. In addition to the Western zodiac, they also sold cards on Egyptian and Chinese astrology. I had not heard of Egyptian astrology before, and learned that each two-week period in the year is under the protection of a different god or goddess, who becomes the guardian deity of those born during that period. My birthday is on 5 July, so I looked up the deity protecting the first half of July: it is the god Anubis.

A UNIVERSAL BLACK GODDESS?

It is also possible that Yemaya's mask has a wider significance than just to tell me who my personal guardian Goddess is. During the last millennium and a half, when the Church drove the old Celtic, Norse, Greek and Egyptian deities underground and starved them of human worship, the Yoruban orishas continued to be worshipped openly and actively. The infamous slave trade took them to the Caribbean and both Americas, and Yemaya became the most powerful of them all, because She protected the slaves on the long sea journey.

Now worshipped by millions of people in Latin America and among the Latinos in the United States, Yemaya may have become the new Isis: the Goddess who subsumes all other goddesses within Herself. To re-establish an equilibrium between our overdeveloped rational and technological minds, and our starved emotions and intuitions, perhaps we Western people need to re-establish not just the worship of a Goddess, but of a Black Goddess from the much abused continent whose exploited people know more than any others what strength there is in sensuality, joy and laughter!

Significantly enough, there is among Italian feminists a cult of Black Virgins, whose altars in old country churches are believed to exude much more power and Goddess energy than the pale complexioned Virgins of ordinary churches.

DRAMA VERSUS RELIGIOUS INTENT

My first wife Gillian died in July 1986. To help me get over my grief my friends invited me to join two other ritual organisations. The first was The Companions of the Rainbow Bridge, a ceremonial ritual training group founded a few years earlier by the high priestess and high priest of my Wiccan coven. The second was the London Iseum of The

Fellowship of Isis, a worldwide Goddess worshipping movement founded in 1976 in Ireland by the Hon. Olivia Robertson and her brother the Earl of Strathloch. I had joined the FoI at its inception in 1976 but had been a purely passive member until then. Both the Rainbow Bridge and the Iseum met once a month, but their rituals could not have been more different.

Rainbow Bridge rituals were very formal and extremely well rehearsed. A formal ceremonial temple was erected in our high priestess' and high priest's sitting room with an altar surrounded on both sides by the pillars Jachim and Boaz. New members were given a Rite of Acceptance that involved a mental journey down the Nile towards a temple of Ra to the accompaniment of gentle mystic music, and had then to adopt a companionship name, preceded by Lady for women, Lord for men.

Everyone wore white robes during formal meetings and only addressed each other by their companionship names while thus robed during the formal meetings. Every meeting enacted a mythical play that one of the members had written, and this play had been well rehearsed on one or two previous evenings after participants had learned their parts by heart, so that on the formal meeting day performance was almost perfect.

The Iseum meetings were completely different. There were no rehearsals and on the days of a meeting members would arrive at my house in their civilian clothes. There copies of a ritual written by Olivia Robertson for the astrological time of the year were handed out. These rituals were written for quite large casts of 30 or 40 actors; as there were only between 8 and 12 of us on each occasion, each of us had to take on three or four different roles. The ritual dramas were then performed by us standing on the same spot in our civilian clothes reading from copies of Olivia Robertson's script.

Yet to my amazement these shambolic unrehearsed rituals had a greater religious impact on me – and apparently on some other members who belonged to both groups – than the beautifully rehearsed rituals of the Rainbow Bridge. Religious intent was apparently more important than dramatic perfection.

THE PERILS OF NEGATIVISM

For the past 30 years I have visited Paris once or twice a year, initially to attend the annual SICOB computer exhibition, and later to give twice yearly computer industry watching seminars. From the beginning I have tried to find local Wiccan groups but met with little success: the local esoteric bookshops offered books on just about every subject from astrology to ceremonial magic, but only one or two on country witchcraft which did not lead me to any active groups.

At last in 1987 someone showed me a small home-edited black and white magazine called *L'Étoile*, which presented itself as the organ of *Wicca française*. Its contents were strange: it devoted a considerable portion of its contents to outraged comments on the Pope's latest rulings (which only affect Catholics) written in a rather vulgar personal manner, e.g. "*Écoute, Jeannot!* ... (Listen Johnny boy!)" Nonetheless I wrote to them and was invited to visit them on a Sunday afternoon during my next visit to Paris in September.

I first met the High Priest, a friendly garrulous middle-aged man called Jacques Coutela who must have been the life and soul of his local bistro. He led me to his apartment where his coven were assembled and I immediately felt the atmosphere to be rather odd. His wife, the High Priestess, who called herself Diane Lucifera, sat brooding silently in a corner with a great black psychic cloud surrounding her. "She is either having a hard time with the menopause," I thought to myself, "or is under heavy tranquillisers, or perhaps the latter because of the first."

The other coven members, all young people, also seemed strangely subdued. English Wiccans tend to be exuberantly joyful in a country where people are normally reserved. French people, on the other hand, are culturally extroverted and often exuberant, but this crowd seemed as repressed as conventional English people. After an hour's conversation, in which Jacques asked me if I knew Anton LaVey (founder of the American Church of Satan), they offered to put on a circle for my benefit, which I gladly accepted.

Their temple was in their loft and its floor was not solid enough to allow any running around, so the ritual was mainly stationary. Six altars were placed around the circle, three for the gods Lucifer, Ashtaroth and Baalzebub, alternating with the three devoted to the goddesses Lilith, Astarte and Diana. Each member of the coven entered the circle individually, prostrating him or herself before each of the six altars and saying in Latin: "I, (personal magical name), dedicate myself to Lucifer/Lilith...etc. unto all eternity." I quickly drew a protective circle around myself and mumbled before each altar saying nothing. Then the coven all together formally renounced their Christian baptism ("They have been doing this for over 15 years every month," I thought to myself, "their renunciations can't have been very effective to have to be repeated so often!"). Then Diane prayed to Lucifer with words that – with names altered – could have come from a Christian prayer book: "Oh Lucifer! You are so powerful and we are so utterly powerless without you. Grant us your protection, and while you are about it, do down those nasty Christians!"

"Have we any work to do?" asked Diane. A young woman, whom one of the members knew, was trying to break from her West Indian lover, but he was trying to retain her with Voodoo magical techniques. Everyone knelt on the floor, put the thumb and next two fingers on the floor in such a way as to touch the fingers of the two people on either side of him or her, and the high priestess then said very quickly: "Listen Josiane, you are in our power, you have nothing to fear. Amen!" and that was it. I did not feel the slightest whiff of a cone of magical power, which was just as well, I thought, since if they had known how to raise it they might have come to real harm with their prayers to Christian demons.

"Well, what do you think of it?" Jacques asked me when we were back in their sitting room. "Interesting," I replied, "but why do you call yourselves Wiccans? Apart from ritual nudity your rituals have nothing in common with English and American Wicca. Why don't you call yourselves *La sorcellerie française* or even better *Le temple de Lucifer*?" "You are wrong," said Jacques, "we are entirely in line with the world wide Wicca movement: a visitor from the USA confirmed this. You can't be very familiar with Wicca." (I later met that American. He had been too polite to comment unfavourably on their rituals, but had certainly not confirmed them as being in the Anglo-American Wiccan tradition.)

As we parted they gave me a copy of their recently published first book called *Douze leçons de magie pratique* (Twelve Practical Magic lessons). I read it in my hotel in the evening. There were among other things the names and prayers to the demons connected with each of the 365 days of the year, and a self-initiation ritual consisting of reciting the Lord's Prayer in Latin backwards. I wrote to them a letter in which I listed all the differences between their and Gardnerian Wiccan rituals, but I never heard from nor met them again.

Yet the negativism of their rituals ended up by taking its toll. In the summer of 1995 I was shocked to learn that Diane, Jacques and their favourite pupil who was living with them had committed suicide. On

55

my next trip to Paris in October I asked a bookseller who had known them well what had happened.

It appears that one of the TV channels had planned a programme on all the magical traditions represented in Paris under the title "Believe it, or believe it not?" and had invited the *Wicca française* team. Diane had been reluctant to participate at first but finally consented, but not without telling the producer that she resented the pressure exercised on them. This annoyed the producer and the interviewer: on the evening of the live performance she put Diane, Jacques and their pupil at the far end of the bench on which all the other magical traditions were seated, and then did not address a single question to them. After 20 minutes of being thus ignored, they walked out of the studio cursing the producer and the interviewer and saying: "You will be sorry for this!"

Three days later Diane called her husband and the pupil together and said: "I see no point in going on!" and then shot herself in front of them. For two days thereafter a distraught Jacques rushed around all his friends and acquaintances saying he could not live without Diane. Then on the third day he and the pupil hanged themselves in the room in which Diane had shot herself.

The bookseller and I speculated that they probably tried to harm the producer and interviewer with black magic, but magically incompetent as they were they drained themselves instead of their own will to live.

What was so destructive about their rituals was not that it was Catholic rituals that they turned on their head, but that they were simply negative. It would have been just as destructive if they had recited the Communist Manifesto backwards. As my mystical experience of cosmic consciousness in January 1958 had taught me, all religions have a portion of the universal truth even though they frequently contradict each other in terms of human logic. Whoever puts his ritual emphasis on denying any religion – as distinct from affirming a different aspect of the universal truth – thereby also denies the ultimate truth of which it is a part.

Their behaviour also confirmed what serious occultists know: the human subconscious, through which we work our spells, works in images and does not understand the negative. The more they renounced their Catholic baptisms and invoked Catholic demons the greater hold Catholic theology and papal pronouncements had on their minds: hence their need to renounce their baptisms at every meeting. They were anything but the free spirits that English and American Wiccans are.

Diane Lucifera and Jacques Coutela did not just harm themselves and their members with their negative rituals: they muddied the name Wicca in France for over 30 years. In a serious French book about occultism the author emphasised that his practices had nothing in common with "those idiots at *Wicca française*." In a French *Encyclopaedia of New Religions, Cults and Sects* published in the 1980s, and which was subsequently translated into German, Wicca is listed as a "fanatical anti-Catholic sect which practises sexual initiation rituals." It is only now, some eight years after the suicide of its HPS and HP, that French groups practising genuine translated Gardnerian rituals dare call themselves again Wicca.

A WRITER'S BLOCK

Many readers will probably have wondered for some time why I did not write earlier about those interesting magical experiences in the late 1950s and early 1960s instead of waiting 45 years to do so.

Goddess knows, I tried to write then. The trouble was that after my experience of cosmic consciousness in January 1958 everything seemed connected with everything else: cosmology + biology + evolution + history + psychology + magic + religion + sexual ethics + economics + politics. I wrote down a project listing just intended chapters and sub-headings: it came to 120 000 words. The Humanist Harold Blackham to whom I showed it told me: "You have enough material there for at least five books. Cut your project up and develop one theme at a time!"

I followed his advice and started a book called *The Relativity of Truth* in which I argued that religions and philosophies should be judged by the effect they have on the behaviour of their adherents. It was hard work but I managed to complete it in the evenings of the eight months I spent in Prague without my family September 1966 to April 1967.

When I returned to London I sent it to three publishers in turn but all rejected it, though one sent me a favourable reader's review. Even my coven friends found it too boring to read. By this time I had become dissatisfied with the book and wanted to amend it, but found myself afflicted with a writer's block that did not affect me when writing professionally about computers.

Trying to understand this blockage I came up with two possible explanations. Either I was running scared away from potential leadership of those searching souls who might come to me – and this thought made me feel really guilty – or I was being held back by a higher power until the time was ripe to publish what had been revealed to me.

The answer came five years later on a business trip to Philadelphia in 1972 to touch base with my employers Auerbach Publishers. Shortly before the trip I read a letter from a Philadelphia witch in *The Waxing Moon* magazine and wrote to her. She replied with an invitation from her high priestess to visit the coven when I was in Philadelphia.

The coven to which she belonged was an Eclectic Celtic one, whose high priestess and high priest had written the teachings and rituals themselves, though no doubt inspired by various things they had read elsewhere. One of their teachings had probably been borrowed in part from Orthodox Judaism's rules about the Kabbalah: "To be a priestess of the Goddess a woman need only be over 18 years old and properly trained. But to be a priest of the Goddess a man must have raised a family."

I have never come across a similar teaching in any other branch of the Craft, but I took it as an answer to the anguished questions I had asked myself about my writer's block. So I forgot about writing religious books for the time being and concentrated on my family life and helping my children with their education.

In 1982 both my son and my daughter completed their polytechnic courses and started their first jobs. Sure enough my writer's block on religious topics lifted and I wrote at first a number of articles for Pagan magazines. Then I wrote a book on my cosmotheology in the form of a new Creation myth, *The Divine Struggle*. I completed it after my first wife's death in 1986 and sent it around to publishers. It was finally published by Nemeton in California in 1990.

THE CENSORIOUS COMPUTER

Early in 1992 I was working on the first draft of what was to become *Religion without Beliefs* when I felt I had to account for the Christian religion's continuing attraction for a minority of teenagers and young people. I engaged in a scurrilous speculation on the possible sexual nature of the sense of sin that made them greet the doctrine of the Redemption with such relief and gratitude. Even as I was keying it in, a little inner voice told me: "This is cheap! You shouldn't be writing this!" But I replied: "Never mind! It's fun! I can show it to my friends and we can have a good laugh, even if I finally delete it before sending the manuscript to a publisher." So I left the passage in and carried on.

About an hour and a half later I felt the time had come to save what I had written. I moved the cursor to the line "Save as..." in the word processing program and clicked. But instead of offering me the usual dialog box in which to put the chapter's name, the computer rebooted thus destroying the previous two hours' writing. Cursing, I started again from scratch and tried to save after three pages: the same thing happened again. I gave up working on the book for the evening.

Two days later I resumed working on the book but in a more serious frame of mind. I left out any scurrilous speculations about young Christians' state of mind and the computer saved my texts in the normal manner. The only time I ever experienced an unrequested boot again was when a distant storm caused an electrical current surge.

TOWARDS INTER-FAITH

The Goddess did not leave it at that. A few days later I received my copy of *The Cauldron* magazine which carried a report of two Christian-Druid meetings that had taken place in previous years. A third was scheduled for three days later. I rang the organiser – Canon Tom Curtis Hayward of Gloucester – whether there were still vacancies: there were and I signed up.

The two day meeting brought together six Christians – two Catholic priests, a Church of Scotland minister, two former missionaries, and a young woman who was also a Druid – six other Druids from two orders, and myself as thirteenth member and the only Wiccan. The atmosphere was extremely friendly and informative. At the end of the meeting, Canon Tom addressed us Pagans and said: "Of course I would rather that you were Christians, but at least you have spiritual paths! In this materialist consumer society the members of all spiritual paths put together are still a minority of the population. We should stick together instead of doing each other down!"

A few days after that, Vivianne Crowley asked me to take her place explaining Paganism and Wicca to an audience of young Evangelical Christians at the Greenbelt Festival, a Christian rock festival in North-amptonshire. It was the last lecture of the festival and some 400 people came to listen. While some asked hostile questions most were friendly and the chairman thanked me for the strength of my convictions and my courage in addressing a Christian audience. A number of listeners asked for my address and one Exeter University student later wrote to me, saying she had recognised her own religious convictions in my description of Paganism and asked for Pagan contacts.

The following winter Olivia Robertson asked me to be part of the Fellowship of Isis delegation to the Parliament of World Religions due to take place in Chicago at the beginning of September 1993. The atmosphere at the Parliament was marvellous, full of goodwill and a common determination to work for the preservation of the environment. All the Christian churches except the Baptists were represented, although the Greek Orthodox walked out half way through, not wishing to share a platform with Pagans and atheistic Buddhists. My guardian Goddess had pushed me into Inter-Faith activities.

MOVING TO AUSTRIA

In the meantime I had got together with my second wife Hildegard but she was not happy in London. At Yule 1993 we visited my father in Austria and resolved to do some househunting. But almost immediately a friend of my father offered us her house to buy, which was ideally situated. It was as if the hand of the Goddess was pushing us to Austria, where we moved in August 1994.

The first six years were lonely from the Pagan point of view, but the absence of the London Pagan social scene gave me more leisure for writing. In 1995 I completed *Religion without Beliefs* about Paganism for a readership of religious anthropologists and liberal Christian theologians: it was published in London in 1997. It contained a short section on Wicca and some of the experiences I have listed in this book.

At last in 2000 we started meeting some Austrian Pagans at a fortnightly pub moot. Then suddenly in the first half of 2003 three Austrian women, one locally and two from Vienna, asked us to initiate them into Wicca. Simultaneously a Gardnerian coven of French students got into touch with me via the Internet and asked me after a couple of meetings with them in France to be their mentor. These simultaneous requests from two directions were the green light of the Goddess to start writing this book about my Wiccan experiences.

6

ACROSS THE POND

Ever since my year with Auerbach Publishers in Philadelphia 1970–1971 I have visited North America on average once a year, with just two three-year gaps from 1977 to 1980 and from 1984 to 1987. I also lived in the San Francisco Bay Area for 15 of the 18 months from December 1987 to June 1989. During these visits I have made many Wiccan and other Pagan friends, mainly in Northern California, but also in Southern California, New York, Boston, Chicago, Wisconsin, Kentucky, Toronto, Vancouver and Seattle.

The American Pagan scene is vibrant and dynamic. The name "Wicca" is used more broadly as a euphemism for all types of witchcraft, and thus covers also totally different spellcasting traditions such as Victor Anderson's Feri or Faery tradition (derived from Hawaian Huna), Starhawk's related Reclaiming tradition, Robert Cochrane's 1734 tradition, the "New Reformed and Orthodox Order of the Golden Dawn" (NROOGD), the Church of All Worlds (CAW) based on Robert Heinlein's novel *Stranger in a Strange Land*, Santeria derived from the Yoruban orisha religion, Circle, Dianic and Eclectic witchcraft, not to mention joke traditions like the Erisians.

Traditions derived from Gerald Gardner's Book of Shadows are called "British Traditional Wicca" (BTW) and there are many more of these than in Britain. In addition to Gardnerian and Alexandrian Wicca, there is also Algard (a mixture of Alexandrian and Gardnerian), Mohsian and Central Valley (of California) Wicca, which includes the Silver Crescent, Majestic, Kingstone and Daoine Coire orders, and whose outer court is called The New Wiccan Church. Gardnerian Wicca is still the largest and most influential tradition and is divided into a number of initiatory lines, the leading ones being Long Island, Kentucky and California.

American Wiccans take their religion very seriously and work hard at it. Nonetheless the non-BTW traditions are often influenced by

Feminist and Gay Liberation political correctness. At one Eclectic circle to which I was invited the participants deliberately did not alternate between men and women around the circle in the Gardnerian manner as this was regarded as "sexist": never mind magical efficacity!

FERI

Some of the home grown American traditions are, however, very powerful. Invited to attend a Feri ritual at the Covenant of the Goddess (COG) Merrymeet festival in September 1987, I witnessed the high priestess become possessed by a deity or entity. Normally a calm and dignified Southern belle, she suddenly starting tearing around the circle at a speed of knots as her whole personality changed.

Intrigued I attended some weekly classes in Feri at her home at the beginning of 1988. There she concentrated on trying to get her leading pupil Dominic to channel Melanctaos, the Peacock God of the Yezidis, a Pagan tribe in South Eastern Turkey called Devil worshippers by their Muslim neighbours. On the first occasion he did indeed channel a deity, but not Melanctaos. Repeatedly flicking his right hand as if he was carrying a fly whisk in the manner of African chiefs I concluded he was possessed by a Yoruban orisha. When he was back in his normal self I asked him whether he practised any other form of witch-craft. "Yes!" he replied, "I also do Santeria."

Later I also took Francesca de Grandis' classes in the Third Road, an outer court introduction to Feri. Even though this was an introductory tradition it was still very powerful. It has a much more direct way for raising power and communicating with elementals than Gardnerian Wicca, but is not for psychically vulnerable people in my opinion. "On the contrary," said Francesca, "you need to be near the edge to do Feri properly!"

CHECKING INITIATORY VALIDITY

In such a multi-traditional environment what does it mean when a person claims to have been initiated, especially after the much read writer Scott Cunningham had written *Wicca, a Guide to the Solitary Practitioner* which includes a "self-initiation" ritual? Americans are moved around the country quite frequently by many employers and Wiccans may land in a remote state or small town where the nearest coven belongs to a different tradition from their own.

As a measure of spiritual quality control Gardnerian covens recognise only Gardnerian initiations performed "in a circle such as I am now in" according to the Book of Shadows. To guard against fraudulent claims from unknown candidates the Long Island family has devised a rather bureaucratic system of checks. Every initiate is given a Certificate of Initiation signed by his or her high priestess as well as photocopies of the high priestess's own certificate and of every other high priestess' in the chain of initiations going back to the first American Gardnerian high priestess Rosemary Buckland. These are irreverently nicknamed "puppy papers". A computerised database of all initiations in the Long Island family is also kept in New York, which Long Island Gardnerian high priestesses can consult if a claimed Gardnerian without the required certificate lands on their doorstep.

To qualify as a Gardnerian initiation every step listed in the Book of Shadows must be followed no matter how symbolically. Covens may add rituals and teachings to their Book of Shadows but must on no account take anything away. One New York high priestess abolished the Binding and Scourging ordeal at her initiations, because it might revive traumatic memories among those who had been physically abused by their parents in their childhood. Her initiations were promptly declared invalid and her initiates not regarded as proper Gardnerians. Her Californian initiates reinstated binding and scourging in their initiations, but those initiates were still not recognised by the Long Island "Hard-Gards" as there had been a break in the line of proper initiations, an Apostolic Succession far more rigorous than that of the Roman Catholic or Orthodox churches.

Yet a Long Island Gardnerian high priestess, whose guest I once was, used "scourges" with thin two-inch handles from which seven strands of soft silk dangled, but her initiates were accepted in the Long Island line, a triumph of ritual formalism over true initiatory experience.

Such mini-scourges are by no means standard issue in the Long Island Gardnerian line. Other covens with whom I have guested had proper cat-o'-nine tails, but the rules of acceptance in that line nonetheless struck me as rather paradoxical.

CROSS-INITIATION

This does not mean that a Wiccan from a different tradition will be automatically refused admission to the only coven there may be in the area to which she or he has just moved. If there is a vacancy in the coven and the applicant is emotionally compatible with the existing members she or he will be offered a "cross-initiation". This tactful term means that the coven is not disputing the validity of their candidate's original initiation in putting her or him in touch with the Goddess and Horned God current, simply insisting that she or he go through the same initiatory experience as the coven's existing members.

Many American Wiccans and other magicians believe, however, that a cross initiation will suffice to put a person in touch with a tradition's spiritual current or egregore even if she or he does not thereafter join a coven belonging to that tradition. During a visit to Southern California in 1980 I was invited to a garden party attended by members of many Pagan traditions, including the founder of the Kabbalistic *Ordo Templis Astartis* (OTA), with whom I got into conversation. After a while he said: "I can recognise a high priest when I see one. Will you trade initiations with me? You initiate one of my priestesses into Gardnerian Wicca and I will initiate you into the OTA!"

As I was due to fly back to London three days later I refused. How could I have learned during that short period what the OTA was all about, or given my OTA friend the experience of working in a Gardnerian coven? "If you ever come to London for a year," I replied, "I will introduce you to my coven and they will initiate you if they like you, but not otherwise!"

A year later I received a similar request from a San Francisco high priestess whom I had seen conduct a seasonal festival of several NROOGD covens and the local OTO branch very competently. Her initiations and training had been Dianic and NROOGD, but she felt a Gardnerian initiation would be much more valid. I again told her our coven might accommodate her if she ever spent a year's work in London.

AIDAN KELLY

Nothing illustrates the pitfalls of cross-initiations better than the case of Aidan Kelly, whose *Crafting the Art of Magic, Part I* (CAMI) published in 1991, was regarded for several years by outsiders as an authoritative history of the origins of Gardnerian Wicca, until it was displaced by

Professor Ronald Hutton's much more seriously researched history *Triumph of the Moon*.

During a university course on Creative Writing in 1968 he had a written a set of rituals suitable for a witchcraft reconstruction group. Many of his fellow students on the course tried his ritual system out and they found that it gave them a feeling of group belonging and of spiritual uplift. So they used them as the basis for the *New Reformed and Orthodox Order of the Golden Dawn* (NROOGD), which became the first witchcraft reconstruction group in the San Francisco Bay area. It was, however, at that time at least, solely a partying tradition which celebrated the seasonal festivals. Years later in 1988 I attended the 20th anniversary NROOGD circle: the circle drawing and quarter invocations were more literary than Gardnerian Book of Shadows ones but did not have the same morphic resonance.

In 1973 Gardnerian Wicca arrived in the San Francisco Bay area and many NROOGD members changed over to it as a more authentic witchcraft tradition because of its spellcasting techniques. Aidan was irritated by this and thought it was the claims of a continuous line of initiations from the Middle Ages which gave it a spurious claim to greater authenticity. So he embarked on a search for original Gardner correspondence at Ripley's and the James (a Canadian Wiccan couple who run a bookshop in Toronto) and submitted Book of Shadows material to textual analysis to prove that Gardnerian Wicca was as much a made up witchcraft reconstruction as NROOGD, just 15 to 30 years older.

In 1977 Aidan discovered that he was alcoholic and joined Alcoholics Anonymous (AA). They told him he needed the support of his religious tradition. As NROOGD members were unable to give this to him he returned to the Catholic faith of his birth, whose local priest was very helpful. But he continued his research into the origins of Gardnerian Wicca. It was during this phase of his life that I visited him in 1981 during a visit to San Francisco to give one of my computer seminars.

He told me that some correspondence between the original members of Gerald's first coven suggested that many Book of Shadows rituals had first been written in the 1950s. "Why, everyone in England knows this!" I replied. It was with some surprise that ten years later I found myself quoted in CAMI as an authority for his thesis that Gerald had invented Gardnerian witchcraft.

I next met Aidan in 1987. By that time he had again left the Catholic church, outraged by the reactionary trends in the Vatican and its silencing of the more progressive thinkers. He had separated from his first wife and had as new companion a fellow AA member: Julie. Finding her psychically dangerously open, he found teaching her to cast Wiccan circles the only way to help her defend herself against dangerous psychic intrusions. But he did not want to go back to NROOGD where he would meet his ex-wife, so asked to join Gardnerian Wicca.

There was no vacancy in the local Gardnerian coven, but thinking him magically competent they gave him a Gardnerian cross-initiation and then the Gardnerian Book of Shadows to copy, and left him free to start a coven of his own.

I spent the summer of 1988 in the San Francisco Bay area and was invited on two occasions by Aidan to Gardnerian rituals, the first at a friend's house, the second at his Alameda home before he moved to New York. On the two occasions Julie did a proper Gardnerian opening but, after the salt and water had been consecrated, followed this immediately with cakes and wine and then closed the circle. "That was a powerful ritual!" she said on the first occasion. Francesca de Grandis from the Feri tradition, another guest, and I looked at each other and exchanged puzzled glances to say: "What power?" There had been no attempt to raise a cone of power nor to engage in any spellcasting.

Well, I thought on the first occasion, Julie is probably still learning, and she must walk before she can run. But the same thing happened at his farewell circle to which many friends, some from as far as Seattle, had been invited. Yet there would have been ample justification to raise a cone of power to protect him and give him luck in his New York job.

I thought at the time that, though Aidan knew how to cast a protective circle, he had no idea of how to raise a cone of power or engage in any form of spellcasting. But in his interview with the authors of *Being a Pagan*, published in 1995 and revised in 2002, he describes participating in a powerful healing ritual for Victor Anderson. However, healing and spellcasting techniques are not described in the Book of Shadows but learned during coven practice. Aidan therefore genuinely believed that the Book of Shadows rituals were all there was to Gardnerian Wicca just as his rituals were initially all there was to NROOGD.

It was therefore perfectly logical for him to assume that, if Gerald and some friends had put together the Book of Shadows rituals, he had invented Gardnerian witchcraft. On that logic Vatican II created a new religion when they replaced the Tridentine Mass by the vernacular Mass. This would not have happened if Aidan had been a member of a real Gardnerian coven after his cross-initiation.

7

WEATHER MAGIC

Although many American Wiccan traditions regard England as the source of all magical wisdom, sometimes American witches are ahead of us. It was not until I circled in America, 30 years after my initiation, that I discovered weather magic although it must have been a stock in trade of genuine country cunning men.

I first came across successful weather magic at the Pagan Spirit Gathering in Wisconsin in June 1988. The whole Middle West was suffering from an oppressive heatwave and drought punctuated by occasional thunderstorms. One had closed Chicago O'Hare airport for three hours on the day of my arrival and my plane had to be diverted to Milwaukee.

At the opening assembly and ritual on a clear cloudless evening we were warned that our camp site was a tinderbox and a spark could set it alight. Fires – a favourite Pagan ritual stage setting – were absolutely forbidden, except in metal containers well off the ground and with a gallon of water close by. At the end of the ritual the Weather Workers of the World (WWW) conducted a weather magic ritual asking the gods to divert our way one of the thunderstorms predicted for North Wisconsin 100 miles from our camp site. Then we all repaired to our tents.

I was woken at 3 a.m. by claps of thunder and a torrential downpour of rain, which my tent fortunately withstood. This went on until 5 a.m. and resumed from 6.0 to 7.30 a.m., leaving the campsite sodden. But by 8 a.m. the sun was shining again and by 10 a.m. the ground was again dry. Later the shopping party who bought food for the whole camp in the nearby town reported there had been no trace of rain within 5 miles of our campsite: the storm had been entirely local.

TAKING OFF FOR PERU

In October 1990, I joined a group of 16 Californian Pagans from the Church of All Worlds on a 10 day trip to the Peruvian temples of the Inca period. We flew from San Francisco to Los Angeles, where we were due to connect with an Argentinian flight to Lima. Five minutes after we landed, fog closed Los Angeles International airport to all landings and takeoffs. There was an enormous queue in front of the Aerolineas Argentinas check-in desk, as the airline was checking nobody in until their aircraft had landed.

Leaving one member of the party to look after our luggage, the rest of us went outside the terminal to a grass knoll and conducted a sympathetic magic ritual to blow the fog away to sea. Within five minutes a light breeze began to blow towards the sea, and after a further five minutes gaps began to appear in the cloud sitting on the airport. We then ended the ritual and returned to the terminal, to find the queue almost gone: they had started checking people in five minutes before.

We still had to wait two hours before the aircraft was ready to take off again. During this time I went to the arrivals hall to reserve a rented car for my return to Los Angeles ten days later. On the arrivals panel, every incoming flight from Latin America except ours was marked as cancelled or diverted.

COMMANDING THE ENGLISH WEATHER

Nine months later, in June 1991, I attended a gathering of some 120 European Wiccans in the English Lake District, one of the most beautiful but also rainiest parts of the country. On the first evening we trudged for ten minutes across fields from our guest house to the meadow where the opening ritual was planned. Apart from the odd cirrus cloud the sky was clear. I was in the outer circle with no ritual role to play.

As the ritual proceeded, my eyes wandered to a tall hill in the south, where I suddenly saw a black thunder cloud emerge from over the hill, heading in our direction. If this goes on, I thought, this cloud will be over us in five minutes, the skies will open and we will be drenched before we can get back to the guest house. So focusing my eyes intently on the cloud I said silently in my head: "Stop! Stay where you are! Respect the boundaries of the circle!" The cloud stopped and stayed in the same spot for five minutes. So I relaxed my concentration and returned to pay attention to the ritual.

After another five minutes, I checked on my cloud to find that wisps of it were beginning to reach in our direction, like a dog which puts first one paw and then another on a bed that he knows he shouldn't climb on. Once more I concentrated on the cloud and held it in its position for the next 20 minutes. It then dispersed to the east and the west, and by the end of the ritual the whole surrounding sky had turned grey, except for that part immediately above our ritual site.

For the next four days we enjoyed dry sunny weather, but on the last day we awoke to find it raining. A Midsummer ritual at a nearby stone circle had been planned for the morning, but was postponed until the afternoon in case the rain stopped. A dozen of us then got together and conducted a weather ritual in the rain, asking the rain to hold off long enough for us to conduct our ritual in the afternoon.

At 1.30 p.m. the rain stopped, and the organisers decided we would hold our planned ritual at the stone circle at 3 p.m. We walked there in dry but cloudy weather, and the ritual started on time at 3 p.m. It lasted 90 minutes and at 4.30 p.m. we closed the circle and returned to our clothes. Five minutes later, it started raining again and went on raining all evening.

KEEPING DRY IN PRAGUE

In September 1997 I attended a conference in Prague on the alchemists and magicians at the court of the emperor Rudolf IV at the end of the 16th century. As we had had unbroken sunny weather in Carinthia all summer I stupidly forgot to take my raincoat on the trip. But when my plane landed in Prague it was raining heavily. I did not, however, catch more than a few drops when boarding a taxi and leaving it at my hotel.

During the course of the afternoon one of our Prague hosts handed out tramway tickets and told us to leave at 6 p.m. on foot to the nearest tram stop which was 8 minutes walk from our hotel. At 5 minutes to 6 it was still raining heavily, so I went on the hotel porch and earnestly asked the rain to stop while we were proceeding to the restaurant. When we left 5 minutes later the rain had stopped. It resumed again while we were eating in the restaurant, but stopped before we left the restaurant for the inaugural meeting. The next two days were bright and sunny.

THE DELAYED HANDFASTING

In June 1998 my wife Hildegard and I were invited to attend the open air handfasting of a couple of friends at the Rollright Stones in Oxfordshire, planned to start at 7.30 p.m. This was to be followed by festivities at a nearby inn. Not wishing to return to London after that, Hildegard and I had booked ourselves into a local bed and breakfast.

The day's weather was not auspicious for an open air ritual. It rained cats and dogs all morning and afternoon as if we were in the tropics. So having checked in to our B&B I donned my raincoat at 4 p.m. and went outside to address the rain. "I know you have an important job to do to irrigate the crops which would die of thirst without you. But surely it won't hurt any crops if you just stop for two hours over the Rollright Stones. So please be kind and stop from 7.30 to 9.30 p.m."

At 7.30 p.m. the officiating high priestess and high priest, the bride-groom and all the guests had gathered at the Rollright Stones and on the dot the rain stopped. But the bride was an hour late and the ritual didn't get under way until 9.0 p.m. We hadn't got very far when at 9.30 p.m. it started raining again and we were drenched by the time the ritual was over.

Moral: Never give such precise times to the weather when you are asking it for a favour. Concentrate on describing the event for which you want dry weather, not the time when it is supposed to be taking place.

WEATHER PUNISHMENTS

The weather does not just react passively to magicians' or witches' requests. It can also act at the request of an angry local deity whose temple or circle has been misused.

THE ANGRY THUNDER GOD

During the tour of the ancient sacred sites and Pagan temples of Peru that I have already mentioned, we spent a day in Lima, and then flew to the former Inca capital of Cuzco, where we spent three days visiting some of the 20 Pagan temples in the hills around the city. These were carved out of natural rock formations during the Inca period or before, so that it was impossible for the Spanish conquerors to destroy them without dynamite, which fortunately they did not possess.

On the second day, we were taken by coach to visit the Thunder God's temple, accompanied by a local shaman – a mestizzo with a university degree in anthropology, who had been impelled by the success of the Carlos Castaneda books in the West to study the old Quechua (the name of the indigenous inhabitants of Peru) religion with village shamen, and was now teaching it to visiting American New Age parties. We were the first Western Pagan group he had met.

It was a clear sunny spring day, quite warm enough to sit in the temple listening to our guide explain the Quechua cosmology, its various gods, goddesses and power animals. After the lecture, he conducted a Quechua ceremony in honour of the Thunder God whose temple we were in.

When he had finished, a woman in our party suggested we show our respect by performing a Church of All Worlds Pagan ritual. Hardly had we gathered in a circle around one of the stones that an angry storm cloud suddenly appeared in the sky to the north, racing towards the temple at the speed of a helicopter. When it was straight above us, it opened up and we were drenched in a downpour of rain. "I feel like going on," said the officiating priestess, and no one demurred. Within seconds, the rain turned to hail, and ice blocks the size of eggs started pelting us. At this point, wisdom prevailed, we broke off the circle and raced back to our bus. Within half a mile, we were back in dry sunny weather: the storm had been purely local.

"This has never happened before," said our shaman guide diplomatically. "It shows the Thunder God recognises you as very special people to be welcoming you in this way!" Some welcome! The god was clearly angry at this inconsiderate misuse of His temple for a ritual that He had not inspired.

THE UNWANTED MEDICINE WHEEL

In April 1997 my wife and I attended a lecture in Villach (Carinthia, Southern Austria) by a local esotericist who had just returned full of enthusiasm from a Sun Bear course in San Francisco. He told us he had been given permission by the Villach city council to erect with volunteers a Lakota Sioux medicine wheel two-thirds of the way up the Dobratsch mountain overlooking the city, at the point where the tarmacadamed road ends. He would be giving a two-day course of the medicine wheel's symbolism in June, just before Midsummer when the wheel was due to be consecrated.

After the lecture I asked the speaker whether he was aware that many Native American tribes object to their rituals being appropriated by white people, and that Sun Bear – a mixed race Native American – is a highly controversial person in the Native American community. The speaker replied he was aware of the controversies surrounding Sun Bear, but the latter had told his audience he (Sun Bear) had been told by God to bring Native American wisdom to Western culture. Since the speaker was blatantly sincere and financially disinterested I let it go.

In mid-June my wife and I attended the two-day introductory course on medicine wheel symbolism. The second day of the course, a Thursday, was dry but windy with heavy black storm clouds being driven across the sky. The speaker asked us to drive up the Dobratsch in the afternoon to help put the stones near their final position on the wheel. As soon as we drove up the mountain it started raining heavily, and we were all drenched by the time we had finished our task of putting the stones in position. Still, given the winds and black storm clouds it might have rained anyway.

Not so on the Saturday when the medicine wheel was due to be inaugurated officially. We awoke to a sunny day with a clear blue sky, with not a cloud in sight throughout the Carinthian valley, except for a single ring of cloud around the Dobratsch mountain at precisely the level of the medicine wheel. The whole inaugural ceremony was once again drenched in rain, with only occasional breaks in the cloud to show us the valley beneath us and the top of the mountain above bathed in glorious sunshine.

Did the Dobratsch mountain spirits object to this alien import? Or did the medicine wheel itself inform them that it wasn't meant to be there? Whatever it was, the rain was anything but accidental.

The medicine wheel is still there seven years later, and it doesn't always rain at its level on the Dobratsch mountain. But it does seem to be cloudy at its level more frequently than on other parts of the mountain.

II

Wiccan Successes
and Failures

8

SUCCESSES

The Wiccan movement's most important success is that it has survived and is still expanding 50 years after the publication of Gerald Gardner's *Witchcraft Today*, 40 years after Gerald's death and 16 years after the death of Alex Sanders who had appointed himself chief publicist after Gerald. From a single coven in 1954 it has spread worldwide through the English speaking world and now also into Continental Europe and now counts possibly anything from 50 000 to 100 000 members. It is true that the name has also expanded to include all spellcasting witchcraft traditions in North America and all Goddess worshippers in Germany, but these movements too hardly existed 50 years ago.

During the same period how many other new religious movements have arisen, had brief moments of growth and publicity, only to shrink into insignificance after their founder's death! What is left of the Rajneeshi movement 12 years after Rajneesh's death? ISKCON is much better healed, with enough money to build magnificent temples in India and many Western countries, but will it continue to expand now that Swami Prabupada has passed on?

Wicca's success in continuing to expand must mean that it meets the spiritual requirements of a growing number of people in the 21st century. Many of these, however, pass on to other practices after a few years: what has disillusioned them? Does Wicca raise more expectations than it can fulfil?

CRITERIA FOR SUCCESS

A religious movement can only be said to succeed or fail in terms of the goals that it has set itself. Wiccans represent the largest component of the membership of the UK Pagan Federation and drafted its three guiding principles a few years ago:

1. Love for and Kinship with Nature. Reverence for the life force and its ever-renewing cycles of life and death.
2. The Pagan Ethic: "If it harms none, do what you will." This is a positive morality expressing the belief in individual responsibility for discovering one's own true nature and developing it fully, in harmony with the outer world and community.
3. Recognition of the Divine, which transcends gender, acknowledging both the female and male aspects of Deity (a somewhat arch formula to accommodate the quasi-Buddhist and humanistic Pagans who do not believe in personal deities).

Within broader Paganism, initiatory Wicca (called Gardnerianism in North America) is a mystery cult whose concept of deity is expressed in *The Charge of the Goddess*. Its salient passages are:

4. "I am the soul of Nature. From Me all things proceed and unto Me they shall return." The Goddess is thus not just within us as living beings, but we are all in Her. One of the aims of some Wiccan rituals is ego transcendence, so as to achieve cosmic consciousness at will and be able to channel those divine energies we call the Earth Mother Goddess and her son and lover the Horned God of Fertility.
5. "All acts of love and pleasure are my rituals": the resacralisation of sexual union, at least when it expresses mutual respect and love.
6. "That which thou seekest, if thou canst not find it within thee, thou willst never find it without thee!" Wicca is thus an experiential religion, in which each of us has to find our truth within ourselves. Our high priestesses and high priests and the authors of books on Wicca are teachers of techniques to find this inner truth, but never teachers of the truth itself.

To these self definitions of the Goddess we should perhaps add this passage from the beginning of the Charge:

7. "There shall ye assemble, Ye who are fain to learn all sorcery yet know not its deepest secrets: to these will I teach things that are yet unknown..."

This identifies Wicca as a dynamic magical craft and not just a passive mystical religious movement.

How far have Wiccans succeeded in achieving these seven aims in our personal lives, as a movement and in the wider society in which we live?

THE RE-EMERGENCE OF GODDESS WORSHIP

As I mentioned in Chapter 1, I had a mystical experience of the Goddess in the arms of my first lover in 1954 and set off to find fellow worshippers in London. The *Society of the Inner Light* admitted only practising Christians and had burned the more pagan of Dion Fortune's unpublished writings. The only pagan Druid order of the time – the *Ancient Druid Order of the Universal Bond* – was and still is heavily patriarchal. The *Fellowship of Isis* was not to be founded for another 22 years. Mary played a very subservient role in Roman Catholic theology and was held up as an example of meekness and obedience to Catholic women. Gerald Gardner's witchcraft was the only game in town for a Goddess worshipper and it comprised only two active covens at the time, into one of which I was initiated.

Contrast the position today. Not only is the Goddess – or multiple goddesses – recognised and invoked by every pagan tradition, including Asatru and all the newer Druid orders; she has penetrated the Christian churches in a big way. The Methodists and the Church of Scotland now routinely invoke God the Father/Mother. Five million Roman Catholic laypersons, priests and even some bishops petitioned the Pope in 1997 to have Mary proclaimed "Co-Redemptrix of the Human Race" on complete equality with Jesus-Christ. Matthew Fox's Creation Spirituality continues to make headway in the underground of all Christian churches, and he has called for a recognition of the Goddess Gaia to balance the male Sky Father. In Catholic Austria, where I now live, references to the Earth Goddess in geomantic workshops cause not a stir.

DIVINE IMMANENCE

For us the Goddess has always been an immanent power within ourselves and the whole of Nature: the Life-Force personified, in contrast to the transcendence of the Jewish-Christian God, who was conceived as so remote from his creation that he incarnated only once in human history in Jesus-Christ.

The concept of divine immanence has made even more progress than the image of the Goddess among Christians. The "Death of God" theologians of the 1960s, having pensioned off the fierce old man in the sky, now find that the only meaningful way in which they can still talk of "God" is as a "force for good within ourselves", though to cover their backs they call this "panentheism" (God is in the world but more than the world) instead of pantheism.

How has this transformation come about? Mainly through the religious wing of the Feminist movement, which adopted the Goddess as a "figure of self-empowerment for women" in the 1970s. They influenced Christian women and made them aware of the sexist language in the Bible and Christian liturgy. Since women have always represented the majority of bums on seats in churches, these had to accommodate them.

But where did the Feminists get the idea of the Goddess from? They could so easily have taken the atheist route and simply dismissed Jehovah as a thought form created by Moses to make the Israelites more repressed and warlike and to keep women in a subservient role. Merlin Stone showed in the 1970s in her book *When God was a Woman* (published in Britain under the title *The Paradise Papers*) that the male Jewish God was preceded in the Middle East and most other parts of the world by a Great Mother Goddess. But she concluded her book by hoping that in the coming age humanity would be able to do without either male gods or female goddesses.

It was from Wicca that the religious Feminists got the idea of the Goddess. Z. Budapest's *Holy Book of Women's Mysteries* plundered the Gardnerian Book of Shadows for its rituals, especially the Charge of the Goddess. And what impressed the Feminists was the charismatic self-confidence that so many Wiccan high priestesses exuded, even in America where women have always been more independent and self-assertive than in Europe. "These women have got something that other women need also." Hence the concept of the Goddess "as an image of self-empowerment for women," whether or not they actually believed in her as a real spiritual power independent of humanity.

And where did Wiccan high priestesses get that self-confidence from? From the image of the Goddess as a divine power equal to the male God, immanent within themselves. From their responsibility as ordained priestesses and coven leaders – and above all, I suspect, from the *Drawing Down the Moon* ritual, an example of the profound effect that a ritual can have in changing human consciousness.

It is true, as Doreen Valiente said in her speech to the Pagan Federation's 1997 conference, that the return of the Goddess and of divine immanence were "ideas whose time had come." But Gerald Gardner and his followers were the first to articulate these ideas openly. Our rituals gave many of our high priestesses charismatic self-confidence, they influenced the religious wing of the Feminist movement, which influenced the Christian churches. And this is something of which we in the Wicca movement have every reason to be proud!

IF IT HARM NONE, DO WHAT YOU WILL!

Unlike the Goddess and divine immanence, the principle of responsible individual moral autonomy antedates Wicca. It goes back at least to the philosophers of the 18th century Enlightenment, and is a cornerstone of Humanism. But in the 1950s you had to be a Humanist to meet fellow believers in moral autonomy, and that meant being an atheist or at least an agnostic. If you wanted a spiritual life you had to sign up to one of the Christian churches or to the Buddhists, and that meant surrendering your moral autonomy and following the precepts of the great founder, be he Gautama the Buddha, Jesus or Paul.

Gerald Gardner's witches were the first to break out of this artificial dichotomy. We proved that it is possible to have a spiritual life, complete with belief in reincarnation, without believing three impossible things before breakfast and without surrendering any of our individual moral autonomy. And we have been followed in this not only by all other branches of Paganism, but by most of the New Age as well.

Do we also live this principle in our lives? I think so. After my Wiccan initiation I became much readier to take risks both in my personal relationships and in my professional life. Three years after my initiation I took the risk of leaving my field of economic research to enter the infant computer industry of which I knew nothing, and I never enjoyed myself so much. Fifteen years later I took another risk in becoming self-employed as a consultant, and again it paid off handsomely.

Statistically the self-employed represent about 10 percent of the English workforce, but more than half of the Wiccans I know seem to be self-employed, not always in the computer industry, but also as psychotherapists, artists, writers, gardeners or oddjob builders. Those who do work for a private or government employer or in a university generally do so in capacities where they can organise their work themselves and see the fruits of their work directly: as computer programmers, teachers or consultants.

Truly most of us seem to do what we will at least professionally. It helps that we seem to be relatively indifferent to money: whether we earn a comfortable living in the computer industry, or struggle as artists, writers or in the ill-paid teaching profession, we don't make a big song and dance about it, and certainly don't judge our success or that of our friends by the money we earn.

However, there is also a substantial minority of Wiccan men who have not discovered their own true will: except in the negative sense that they don't want to work in any bureaucracy, nor in industry or commerce. They then live on the borderline of penury and often become psychologically addicted to cannabis.

PRESERVING THE ART OF SPELLCASTING

Gerald Gardner's main aim in publicising his version of witchcraft was to find new recruits who would preserve the ancient art of spellcasting: to heal others and ourselves as well as to improve their and our chances in life by the power of the focused minds of a coven alone.

In this, Gardnerian Wicca has certainly succeeded. I described the results of two remarkable spells in Chapter 3 of this book, and many more in my book *Religion without Beliefs*. The occasional requests for healing energy on the Internet and the readiness with which Wiccans respond to these makes me feel that the art of spellcasting is alive and well in other covens as well: and it wouldn't be if the members of those covens hadn't found that most of their spells achieve the desired results within a comparatively short length of time.

Belief and competence in spellcasting is not universal in the wider Pagan community. In 1988 the now long since defunct American magazine *Fire Heart* conducted a round table discussion between four well known Pagans on the subject of Magical Ethics. Three of them did not really address the question because they thought that magical spells affect only the state of mind of the magician casting the spell – an unsurprising scepticism considering the uniquely rationalist and materialist society in which we live. All the more credit for Wicca to have revived this ancient art and to be generally so good at it.

9

HOW CLOSE ARE WE TO NATURE?

Love for, and kinship for, Nature is the most important of the UK Pagan Federation's three principles and of Wiccan goals as well, since we worship and not just revere Nature, and because humanity's survival depends on it. Unless the whole of humanity can once more feel part of Nature instead of standing outside it and trying to dominate it, we are heading for an ecological catastrophe which could endanger the survival of the human race. If that occurs, it will spare no one: Goddess worshippers and pantheists will go under side by side with unreformed patriarchal monotheists, atheists and materialists. Yet in this most important respect our record is distinctly mixed.

This may seem a surprising assessment, since ecological awareness is rising all the time among the general public. Forty-six years ago it wasn't an issue, even apparently for Gerald Gardner who distrusted elementals and advised us to keep away from them. Today every government, except the Bush administration in the USA, and many industrial firms feel the need to proclaim their concern for ecology, even though it is often no more than lip service.

Agreed, but that wasn't our doing. The prime motivators have been the Club of Rome report in 1972, and since then campaigning by secular movements like Friends of the Earth and Greenpeace. I am not complaining about this: we can't be at the origin of all worth-while developments. The age of monolithic religious movements dictating all human behaviour is past, thank Goddess: the ethic of the coming age is a patchwork quilt with many contributors. We have contributed Goddess consciousness, divine immanence and a revived interest in magic and spellcasting: that is quite enough for a small movement.

The real question is: Are we as individuals and a movement closer to Nature than our non-Pagan neighbours, especially since the opportunity to worship Nature in common is probably what attracts most new recruits to Paganism and eventually Wicca?

POSITIVE FEATURES

On the positive side, few if any Wiccans and other Pagans are active polluters. We tend to walk to nearby shops rather than take the car for short distances, use public transport wherever available, keep our cars and other consumer durables as long as they give good service instead of exchanging them frequently for the latest fashionable models. We treat our cars as convenient means of personal transport, not as badges of professional success and social prestige, and don't therefore run any that are larger and more energy consuming than strictly necessary.

Many of us are active for environmental causes. Two Pagan movements – the Dongas Tribe and DRAGON – played a leading role in seeking to obstruct the desecration of Twyford Down in Hampshire for the M3 extension, as well as the demolition of homes for the M11 extension. Their efforts greatly increased the costs of these two motorway extensions and probably caused the government of the time to abandon plans to drive a similar motorway through Oxleas Wood in Kent. In North America, many Pagans are active members of Earth First, who demonstrate against the clearcutting of California's ancient sequoia forests.

Finally many more covens than 30 years ago hold sabbats, initiations and even full moon magical meetings out of doors: on private property when they have access to it, but even in public woods at night when the last dogwalkers have gone home.

FAILURES

But the majority of Wiccans and Pagans don't seem to have grasped that charity begins at home, and that the parts of Nature closest to us are:

1. our own bodies,
2. our children,
3. the trees and plants in our gardens and neighbourhoods, and the elemental spirits that dwell in them.

As the Green movements always say: Think globally, but act locally!"

1. Caring for our bodies

Some of us look after ourselves properly, perhaps everyone reading this book does, but then so do quite a few country vicars, atheist philosophers and ordinary members of the public. But looking at the movement as a whole, there is no sign that on average Wiccans and other Pagans live healthier lives than our non-Pagan neighbours.

Take smoking. Forty years have elapsed since the US Surgeon-General's report linking chain smoking to lung cancer, but well before that it was well known that heavy smoking could cause respiratory and heart problems. Yet Wiccans and other Pagans smoke as much or as little as their colleagues and neighbours: hardly at all among the academics, computer experts, management consultants and psychotherapists living in leafy suburbs; but still heavily in working class areas like South London. At *The Secret Chiefs* (formerly *Talking Stick*), London's leading Pagan pub moot, non-smokers can get through a year's worth of passive smoking in a single evening.

Just as enjoying a glass of wine or beer with a meal does not make one an alcoholic, so smoking the odd cigarette at a party once a week to keep friends company, or enjoying a cigar after a formal dinner, does not make one a tobacco addict. It is the chain smokers who need a cigarette every 30 minutes or so who are the addicts, who pollute the atmosphere for their neighbours and run a great danger of lung cancer or heart disease as soon as their consumption exceeds 10 per day. I have met too many of these in Wicca, some even smoking in the Circle

In the United States, pressure against smoking in public is so much more intense than in Europe that many Americans have taken up over-eating as an alternative stress reliever. The result is that a large proportion of Americans suffer from a degree of clinical obesity – sorry, horizontal challenge – that one sees in Europe only rarely, and then only among sufferers of thyroid imbalance. At the Covenant of the Goddess Merry-meet in September 1993, a good quarter of the attendees (all initiated Wiccans) were in that category, and a car shuttle had to be organised to ferry them to a ritual site 200 metres away.

I am not referring to the normal tubbiness of many middle aged men (myself included) and women who can be perfectly healthy and dynamically active with it. Least of all am I erecting (as one woman accused me at a lecture once) Vogue models and Playboy playmates as ideal bodies for women to aspire to. When I talk of obesity, I mean people who look as if they weigh more than 140 kilos (300 lbs), who are out of breath after walking ten paces.

Now I am well aware that smoking as well as overeating are stress relievers, and that people who live on social security or boring jobs with low wages in rundown public housing estates, where drug dealing and crime is rife, have rather more stress to cope with than people with well paid stimulating jobs living in middle class suburbs. Similarly, people living in the United States, especially the hyperactive and hyper-competitive East Coast, where there is no ceiling to the financial rewards of success, but no floor below which the losers cannot fall, suffer more stress than people living in the more highly taxed but more socially cushioned Europe. But what are all our meditation and magical techniques for if not to help us reduce our stress and improve our professional and living conditions without endangering our health?

"Fred, why are you talking like a pompous prat?" Maxine asked me after I had made these point in a lecture to a Pagan Federation conference. So let me make it clear that I am not trying to set myself up as an authority on what and how much Wiccans may eat, drink and smoke. I am merely pointing out that we are all part of Nature and not standing outside it. As a well known Pagan song puts it:

"We all come from the Goddess and to Her we shall return
Like a drop of rain flowing to the ocean."

If too many of these drops are polluted then the ocean itself becomes polluted. And if we surrender our freedom of action to one or more addictions, how can we channel any of our goddesses and gods?

2. Raising children

If in looking after our own health we are no better but no worse than our non-Pagan neighbours, when it comes to raising families we seem to be worse. Not in the treatment of our children, whom all the Wiccan and Pagan parents I know treat with respect, affection and tenderness, but in our willingness to have them at all.

Leaving out all young people in their 20s who are still at the experimental stage in their relationships and counting only Wiccan couples who have been together more than 5 years and look set for the long haul, I reckon that no more than one in four Wiccan couples whom I know in Britain have children, and most of these have only one. That works out at an average Wiccan family size of 0.25 children compared to a European average of 1.8, which is itself below the replacement level.

Now it may well be that there are a much larger number of less visible Wiccan parents, because while caring for small children they have less leisure to attend Pagan pub moots, Wiccan gatherings or even their local coven. My first wife and I were also much less active and visible when our children were small. But we would need six invisible for every visible Wiccan family with children to bring the average Wiccan family size up to the European average.

Once again, please don't get me wrong. I am not joining conservative patriarchal monotheists in saying that it is the duty of every couple to have children. Children need lots of attention, love and tolerance from their parents, and only adults who really love children can give them that love. So if you don't like children, you are right not to have them. What concerns me is that only a minority of mature Wiccans seem to be child lovers, which is one of the signs of feeling part of the life-stream.

Some Wiccans and Pagans justify their childlessness as "being responsible: The world is overpopulated as it is." Humbug! Asians, Africans and Latin Americans may be outbreeding their natural resources, but Europeans and North Americans are not. If the average size of the European family remains at 1.8 children, the Western European population is set to decline by 10% over the next 30 years in the absence of large scale immigration from the Third World, which would encourage racism and fascism among the poorer Europeans.

Some large metropoles – London, New York, Los Angeles – and the Dutch North Sea coast may be overpopulated, but the rest of North America and Europe are not, since we produce far more food than our populations can consume, and we would still produce enough food if our farmers abandoned intensive farming methods and returned to ecologically friendly farming.

Do you really think it is in Gaia's interest that the best educated and most tolerant sections of the population should remain childless, and leave all the breeding to fanatical monotheist fundamentalists and the illiterate poor? There is of course no guarantee that the children of Wiccan and other Pagan parents will themselves practise Paganism: indeed a majority of them probably will not. But if brought up lovingly and tolerantly, most of them will grow up to be equally open minded, tolerant and hopefully environmentally responsible.

3. Closeness to trees, plants and elementals

Don't even ask! I have met natural psychics who can see elemental spirits in the forest and the countryside, but few in Gardnerian and Alexandrian Wicca. There are Pagan magical traditions that try to teach their trainees to develop such awareness – Victor Anderson's Faery tradition in California for instance – but Wicca isn't one of them.

After 20 years of solitary magical workings in the wood near my London home I can feel and hear – but not see – elemental spirits. And it was from Californian friends in the Church of All Worlds that I learned to converse with the clouds and to do weather magic, which many of my English Wiccan friends treat with scepticism.

4. All Acts of Love and Pleasure

In the 1950s, when I was initiated, patriarchal sexual mores still prevailed officially in Britain. Couples living together without benefit of clergy were still described as "living in sin" and had to conceal this from their parents and relatives so as not to upset them. Censorship prevailed on all forms of erotic art and literature, which were described as obscene and "liable to deprave and corrupt" those who viewed or read them.

In this atmosphere Wiccan covens joined the Progressive disciples of Bertrand Russell and H. G. Wells in being radically counter-cultural. Not only did all our couples live together for long periods of time before embarking on marriage, but our relationships were very open at least within our covens. Sexual intimacy was regarded as appropriate not only in expressing the mutual love of a committed couple but also close friendships. More than 10 years before the flower child period of the late 1960s we already lived their values.

How different the situation is today! Western society has become much more tolerant. It is taken for granted that couples will live together before getting married, and a diminishing minority of people take offence at gay or lesbian couples. But if society as a whole has moved in our direction, Wiccans and other Pagans have met it half-way.

Like our non-Pagan neighbours younger Wiccans and Pagans practise serial monogamy before marriage, with only one intimate relationship at a time. A new love must be preceded by breaking off the previous relationship even if this was going well, and despite the hurt this can cause the deserted partner. Only in California do some Pagans still experiment with polyamorous relationships and explore concepts like religious orgies and sacred prostitution.

I have not mentioned our collective failure to live closer to Nature to induce guilt feelings. Neither Wicca nor the broader Paganism are guilt-driven religions, and guilt has been ineffective in making Protestant Christians live more loving and socially responsible lives. I am establishing facts so that we may look for the causes.

To feel part of Nature instead of as isolated individuals requires a change of consciousness, which is the purpose of our rituals. Why have these, so effective in raising the self-confidence of our high priestesses and in making most of us recognise and act on our own true wills, failed so dramatically in making us more body- and Nature-conscious? Have we got the right rituals but are not performing them properly? Or have we got the wrong rituals for this particular purpose?

SEASONAL RITUALS

The four grand Sabbats of Wicca – Imbolc, Beltane, Lammas or Lughnasad, and Samhain or Halloween – are meant to reconnect us spiritually with our Pagan farming ancestors, and at the same time make us identify more with the annual cycle of the seasons. But most Wiccans, as well as the wider Pagan community since these are open non-oathbound rituals, frustrate this purpose by timing them always on the Saturday night closest to 31 January, 30 April, 31 July and 31 October irrespective of the climate in which we live and of the weather, because those are the dates given in the Book of Shadows and repeated in books by the Farrars and others. To follow books rather than the Nature around us is a hangover from scriptural religion, that should have no place in a Nature-oriented religion.

Now the Pagan ancestors with whom we are trying to reconnect, be they Celts, Saxons or Norse, were mostly illiterate farmers and you can be sure they did not time their seasonal festivals according to dates in the Julian or Gregorian calendar laid down in some book. Farming alternates between periods of intense activity and others when comparatively little needs to be done. When a period of intense activity ended, the farmers used to have a great big party and that was what the major Sabbats were.

Imbolc or Candlemass celebrated the end of the winter ploughing season and of lambing in sheep-raising districts, and this varies from year to year according to the severity of the winter and the onset of thawing, and even more between climatic zones.

Beltane or Walpurgisnight was a fertility orgy that took place when the nights had become warm enough to make love out of doors: anything from Easter in the eastern Mediterranean to Midsummer in Scandinavia, but mostly some time in May in southern England and central Europe.

Lammas or Lughnasad celebrated the successful end of the harvest – any time between late July and mid-August in cereal growing districts depending on how dry or wet the summer had been, but towards the end of September in vine and other fruit growing districts.

Finally, **Samhain** or Halloween was a food orgy at the onset of winter, in which the village people ate the meat of all the animals they had had to slaughter because there was not enough feed for them to last through the winter, and they were roasted on bonfires that used up the wood of dead branches.

Most, though by no means all, contemporary Wiccans live in large cities where it is difficult to know what happening on farms, but that doesn't absolve us from observing the nature that surrounds us. How about using the flowering of the first snowdrops or some other winter flower to time Imbolc?

When I lived in the Hampstead Garden Suburb north of London, the flowering of the cherry trees along the suburb's streets always marked the height of spring for me: mostly around the beginning of May, but as early as late March or early April after mild winters when spring comes early, or as late as the middle or end of May when spring has been very cold.

School summer vacations have traditionally been timed to coincide with the harvest, and give even city dwellers the leisure to take a trip into the countryside to see what is going on. And most of us live near enough to some park or wood where we can observe when the dead leaves start falling off trees.

If the rigidity with which we time the four great Sabbats takes no account of vagaries of the weather from one year to another, still their dates do correspond roughly to the cycle of the seasons in southern England. But they become downright absurd when transposed to the totally different climates of the southern part of the USA or of Australia.

Yet the only coven I know that has redefined its seasonal festivals to take account of the local climate is the Roebuck coven in Los Angeles (which belongs to the Robert Cochrane 1734 tradition). They live in a near desert where the vegetation dies and turns brown at the height of the summer but revives when the rains come on in November. So they celebrate the festival of Death at midsummer and the birth of the new vegetation year at the beginning of November. This is the sort of creative adaptation to local climatic conditions that every coven should do.

CALLING THE QUARTERS

Another ritual that was designed to bring us closer to the Earth around us is the calling of the Quarters at the beginning of each Wiccan and Pagan circle, and bidding them farewell at the end. In Gerald Gardner's original coven, we just invoked East, South, West and North after checking with a compass in which direction they truly were, but it was not long before covens associated each of the four elements with one of the quarters.

Once again, most Wiccan covens and Pagan gatherings have frustrated the purpose of this ritual by letting books rather than the geography of the place determine which element is associated with which quarter. So from Norway and Scotland to France, and from Germany to Southern California we invoke Air in the East, Fire in the South, Water in the West, and Earth in the North. Only the Australians have reluctantly agreed that to invoke Fire in the South is absurd in the Southern Hemisphere when the midday sun is quite clearly in the North, and they have therefore reversed the attributions of Fire and Earth. But it is just as absurd to invoke Water in the West when you live on the eastern seaboard of the United States, or for that matter on the English east coast.

Nor are these elemental attributions common to all Nature religions. According to a course I once attended near San Francisco, the Navajo of New Mexico put Air in the North, Fire in the East, Water in the South and Earth in the West.

UNSUITABLE RITUALS?

Whereas the seasonal sabbaths and the calling of the quarters are quite suitable for bringing us closer to Nature and fail only because we are not performing them properly, there are other rituals that may themselves be counter-productive and alienate us from Nature instead of bringing us closer to the Life-Force.

When Gerald Gardner wrote *Witchcraft Today* it was to recruit new members into the witchcraft tradition to replace those from traditional witchcraft families who were dropping out. But he felt that people coming from the outside, from an ultra-materialist and rationalist society with no family history of magic behind them, needed initially at least some pretty heavy ritual to put them into an altered state of consciousness in which they might be ready to try spellcasting and magic.

According to Gerald the rituals of the New Forest coven, into which he had been initiated in 1939, had been "rather sketchy", which probably means that like contemporary Eclectics they made them up as they went along, and tried them out to see if they would work. Not being ritually creative himself, Gerald turned for rituals to the tradition into which he had been initiated 30 years before he discovered the New Forest coven: Freemasonry. Although I have never been a Freemason myself, the 1st degree initiation sounds masonic, including the bit where the initiate is pulled along with a towrope, and the use of the term "the Craft" to describe our tradition.

Gerald supplemented masonic rituals with others taken from the Greater Key of Solomon (GKS). Gerald took those rituals because they sounded good when declaimed, and they certainly have several centuries of morphic resonance behind them. But he never paused to think whether they were compatible with the polarity-oriented pantheistic Goddess and God theology that he was teaching, and simply took them as they stood. I have already mentioned the shock I got when, at my first degree, the coven sword was presented to me with the words: "With this in your hands you can command angels and demons...." "Angels and demons!" I thought "what are they doing in what is supposed to be a non-dualist religion? Gerald must be theologically illiterate!"

Freemasonry originated in 16th century Scotland. GKS was part of the tradition of Renaissance Magic. Both aim to make the initiate self-reliant and free him from subservience to the Roman Church hierarchy, but both share the Christian world view that the rational intellect is man's highest feature and the only one made in the image of God (or the *Logos* as Western Mysteries initiates would say). Subjective feelings on the other hand are to be distrusted and kept strictly under the control of the rational mind. It is true that Renaissance magicians were closer to Nature than we are, but they were trying to dominate it. Out of their magic came modern science and technology, which centuries later has produced the society in which we live.

The Presentation of the Tools

If you don't believe me, consider the presentation of the tools in the 1st degree initiation. Although the Book of Shadows does not state it, each tool symbolises one of the four elements. We begin by being presented with no less than three steel cutting objects: the **sword**, the **athame** and the **white handled knife**, all representing Air, i.e. the conscious rational intellect, which analyses (= cuts) reality into segments that fit into pre-ordained categories. (Personally I have always felt they represent rather the element of Fire, i.e. willpower, but that is a minority opinion among magicians.) Whether they represent Air or Fire, they represent a "male" element and they are heavily over-emphasised.

I thought at the time that this was due to Gerald's fascination with knives: his first book was after all a treatise on the magical uses of the Malayan *kris*. But my high priestess of the time put me right: in the

Greater Key of Solomon the initiate is presented with no less than 10 different types of knife and sword (including the poignard – I forget the others).

If the sword and knives represent Air and therefore intellect, the **wand** represents Fire and therefore willpower. The **pentacle** represents Earth and material possessions, and the **censer of incense** represents Spirit. But not a single tool is presented at initiation to represent Water, the element of feelings and love. We use the **cup** in the circle, but it is not presented to the initiate as a worthwhile tool at 1st degree initiation in the original Gardnerian Book of Shadows, though some covens may subsequently have added it.

I have heard several explanations for this omission but none that make any sense to me. When asked about this omission, Gerald said that it had astonished him too when he was first initiated. The reason was that if, during the persecutions, a witch was found with her tools and these included the cup, the inquisitors would think that witches had a ritual profaning the Christian Mass and they would be tortured worse as a result.

But in the Book of Shadows it also states that witches should only use ordinary kitchen utensils as tools, which any farmer's wife would have. Surely even the lowliest peasant had a cup from which to drink water or beer, so why would a cup found in the possession of an accused witch be incriminating? A sword would be a far worse thing to be found in the possession of a farmer, identifying him as a potential rebel if not as a witch.

This is just the sort of cock and bull story Gerald would have thought of on the spot, because he wouldn't have been willing to admit he had lifted the initiation ritual from Freemasonry or the Greater Key of Solomon and not noticed the omission of the cup.

A rather more sensitive explanation is that the cup is not a tool at all, but the Craft's central mystery representing the womb of the Goddess. Fair enough, but why not present it to the first degree initiate as a symbol of the mystery rather than as a magical tool? After all, he would soon be drinking from it during cakes and wine.

The Blessing of the Elements

If you think this omission of the Cup and therefore of the element of Water at 1st degree initiation is accidental, consider the Blessing of the Elements that we perform whenever we open a circle, at least at closed Wiccan Full Moon meetings.

"I exorcise thee, oh Creature of Water, that thou cast out from thee the impurities and uncleanesses of the world of phantasm!" What could these impurities and uncleannesses possibly be: sexy thoughts, perhaps, about one of the attractive women or men standing opposite you in the circle? How would you feel, if this phrase was translated into modern idiom as: "I exorcise thee, oh Feeling of Love, that you cast out from yourself all impure and unclean sexual desire and imagination!"

Nor, having been exorcised in this way, does Water then receive any blessing on its own. First the salt – representing the element of Earth, and therefore material possessions – is addressed in a much more positive way: "Blessings be upon this Creature of Salt! Let all malignity be cast from thencefrom and all purity enter herein!" The High Priestess then casts salt into the water, and only then blesses the water, saying: "Wherefore do I bless thee and invoke thee that thou mayest aid me." Supposing instead of salt being cast into the water, we cast consecrated monetary coins into the water with the same words?

At best, this symbolism says: "Don't let passion turn your head and make your loved one pregnant before you have earned enough material possessions to provide her and her children with a secure home!" At worst: "Don't marry for love, but only for a consolidation of adjacent properties, two businesses or two kingdoms!", which is how marriages are still arranged in Asia, and were in Mediterranean countries until two generations ago.

During a discussion on this very topic at a Wiccan gathering someone said the "impurities and uncleannesses of the world of phantasm" were arrogant self-aggrandisement in thought and building unrealistic castles in the air. But such megalomania in thought would belong to the element of air, not the element of water.

As for the altar candle (Fire) and the censer of incense (Air or Spirit), no need to either exorcise or bless them! They are male and represent willpower and the intellect, and are therefore pure and holy by their very nature! As if intellect and willpower uninformed by love and feeling could not be unutterably cruel as in the Inquisition, Nazism and Communism!

There is actually a more humdrum explanation for their omission. The ritual for the blessing of the elements was copied by Gerald or someone in the New Forest coven from the Greater Key of Solomon ritual for the preparation of the magician's ritual bath before opening the Temple, and of course in any bath you need only water and maybe bath salts. But taken out of the context of a ritual bath and introduced into the opening of the circle, it does have all the above negative suggestions.

A Language of Command and Aggression

Most other Gardnerian rituals taken from Masonry or the Greater Key of Solomon are full of words of command and aggression:

"I summon, stir and call ye up, ye Mighty Ones of the (East, South, West, North)",
"With this in your hand, you can *command* angels and demons!",
"The athame is the true witch's *weapon!*"
and so on.

Don't think that just because you don't understand their symbolism when you perform them these rituals can't affect you! The less you understand them consciously, the more effectively they will shape your unconscious.

THE CAUSE OF OUR SUCCESSES AND FAILURES

When we consider the thrust of this ritual language, we can understand both our successes and failures as a movement. The overemphasis on the tools that symbolise intellect and willpower has given our initiates of both genders stronger egos, more self-confidence and – among our high priestesses – a great deal of charisma. It has helped most of us recognise and act on our own true wills: hence the high proportion of self-employed people among us.

It has also given many of us the curiosity and self-confidence to enter the computer industry, a high-tech industry of the future if ever there was one, but one with such a rip-roaring rate of constant change that one needs a great deal of self-confidence to be able to keep up with it.

However, in strengthening our egos these rituals also imprison us further in our time- and space-bound individual consciousness and alienate us further from the life-stream, further perhaps even than most of our non-initiated contemporaries. That is probably why we as a movement not only do not look after our health better than our non-Pagan neighbours, but we also seem to be a great deal less interested than them in having children. For to have children and bring them up properly means sacrificing a great deal of personal time and freedom for the sake of seeing life through their younger, more innocent and questioning eyes, and for keeping life going after our own individual deaths.

10

THE ELUSIVE
EGO-TRANSCENDENCE

Initiatory Wicca is supposed to be more than the reverence of Nature that it shares with all other Pagan traditions. It is supposed to be a "craft" of spell casting to help ourselves and others with the power of our focused minds. In this, as I have mentioned above, Wicca has generally succeeded. Most covens can cast spells quite effectively, especially when trying to heal themselves or their friends, and quite a few initiated Wiccans can also cast effective spells on their own.

But Wicca goes further. At least our 3rd degree high priestesses should be able to transcend their own egos and achieve cosmic consciousness when the Moon is called down on them, from which vantage point they should then be able to channel the Goddess' specific advice to their coven and its individual members. The "Charge of the Goddess" is meant to be a standby text to be recited when for whatever reason the Goddess doesn't come through. Such ego-transcendence is supposed to be a condition for the 3rd degree, which in turn is a precondition for being allowed to hive off and start her own coven.

It is easy to see why. Anyone who has ever achieved cosmic consciousness (the Hindus call it "enlightenment"), be it through a spontaneous mystical experience or as a result of meditation or other spiritual exercises, thereafter finds personal preoccupations with one's own recognition by others, prestige, power and so on insignificant compared with the wonderful immensity of the universe she or he has just experienced.

A high priestess able to channel the Goddess will thus tend to be a charismatic but tactful leader of her coven, able and willing to listen to everyone's point of view before articulating a true consensus of the coven as a whole. She will also be in a good position to instruct other coven members to achieve the same ego-transcendence.

I have been a member of two covens in London and have guested with three other English covens, three Continental covens as well as at least three covens in the United States and one in Canada. Yet I have hardly ever witnessed the high priestess truly channel the Goddess when the Moon was called down on her, at least not to the extent of going into trance and channelling the Goddess' own specific advice to individual coven members. Each time the Charge was recited from beginning to end, a truly moving piece of ritual poetry that never fails to bring tears to my eyes, but channelling the Goddess it isn't.

My own high priestess of 20 years and several others with whom I guested were nonetheless quietly strong but tactful leaders of their covens, able to create a loving family atmosphere in the coven. But I suspect that much of the bitchcraft between some covens and their high priestesses on both sides of the Atlantic was the result of clashes between untranscended egos.

Once again, did we not have the right rituals to lead us to ego-transcendence? Or do we have them and are just not performing them properly?

RITUAL NUDITY

There are in fact several ritual techniques in Wicca that should help us transcend the boundaries of our egos: the first is ritual nudity.

Whenever we wear clothes of any kind we create personas for ourselves behind which we hide our true selves. When I gave seminars on the latest developments in computer technology to the information system managers of large firms and local authorities I wore a sober dark suit, a white shirt and a tie. It made me feel the responsible expert that I was and I was recognised as such by my audience. At Pagan pub moots, on the other hand, or when hiking in the countryside, I wear comfortable informal clothes: jeans, an open-necked shirt and – in winter – a pullover. When magicians wear ritual robes they also create a persona for themselves – the magician – quite different from their everyday working or family persona, but a persona nonetheless.

It is only when we cast off all our clothes that we show ourselves truly as Mother Nature has made us. This implies trust in those with whom we are naked, who in turn thereby express their trust in us. Ritual nudity is thus an important contributor to the closeness of the human relations in most covens. It also happens to be the most comfortable way in which to run around to empower spells!

There is a further reason for this: to express in practical ways our conviction that the human body is sacred and a fit embodiment of the divine energy within us after centuries of sensual repression by the Christian churches and other patriarchal monotheistic religions.

As a student active in promoting European federalism I was invited in April 1951 to attend a gathering of federalist students from several European countries on the Ile de Port-Cros off Toulon, organised by the Conférence Olivaint, a Jesuit organisation for training the sons of rich French bourgeois families for politics. A neighouring island is the Ile du Levant, the oldest public nudist island. So during a discussion I once asked one of the Jesuit priests why the Catholic Church forbade nudism, since it was well established that complete nudity is much less conducive to "sinning" than the wearing of bikinis.

The priest laughed and said: "Sinning is human. We don't object to people sinning as long as they are aware of their sin and sincerely try after confession not to do it again. But the public display of the naked human body is tantamount to a doctrinal affirmation of the innocence of the Flesh, and that is heresy!" It is precisely this affirmation that we make through ritual nudity.

All the Wiccan covens to which I have belonged and with which I have guested have been faithful to the practice of ritual nudity. This has also made most of their members – though not all – sufficiently comfortable with their bodies to enjoy naked sunbathing and swimming outside the circle when given the opportunity, though rarely sufficiently keen to join a nudist club. At one annual Wiccan gathering the naked disco has become quite a tradition.

It disturbs me, however, that a growing number of newer Wiccan covens choose to wear robes during their magical workings, because they have found that nudity isn't necessary to cast successful spells. Of course it isn't – nor is the wearing of magical robes: you can cast spells quite effectively in ordinary civilian clothes once you have mastered magical techniques, but that isn't the point.

THE EIGHTFOLD PATH

The Gardnerian Book of Shadows lists eight other techniques for raising power to cast successful spells. All of them can, if persisted in long enough, also result in a mystical experience of ego-transcendence and cosmic consciousness.

1. Meditation or concentration,
2. Trance states (actually more an aim than a method),

3. Drugs, wine and incense,
4. Dancing,
5. Chants and spells (in the sense of rhyming ditties),
6. Blood and breath control,
7. Scourging,
8. The Great Rite.

These are not meant to be exclusive. Other techniques, not listed in the Book of Shadows, might include:

9. Drumming,
10. Eastern techniques like Reiki, etc.,
11. Dervish dancing in circles around one's own axis,
12. Amerindian sweatlodges or Nordic saunas.

As a lifelong asthmatic Gerald Gardner could not dance energetically and had to be very careful with alcoholic drinks and breathing in an incense-filled atmosphere. He disapproved of drugs. He had a tin ear so that chants, spells, drumming and any other form of music wouldn't do much for him. By a process of elimination, therefore, the only techniques that worked for him were a combination of mental concentration, blood and breath control through binding, and scourging, and these were the techniques he taught us and have been perpetuated in Wiccan rituals.

BINDING AND SCOURGING

I have already mentioned in Chapter 3 that under Gerald's influence the Bricket Wood coven initially used binding and scourging not only at 1st and 2nd degree initiations, but also for "purification" at the beginning of meetings and to raise power when working magic.

It was something of an obsession with Gerald in the way he structured the 2nd degree elevation and the references he introduced into several rituals. In the blessing of the salt and the water he added: "Mindful that water purifies the body, but the scourge purifies the soul." In the Charge of the Goddess he added: "At mine altars, the youths of Lacedaemon and Sparta paid due sacrifice", a reference to a competition during the festival of Artemis in ancient Sparta (Lacedaemon is just another name for the same city) between young men aged 16 to 18 as to who could endure being whipped longest without flinching or fainting, during which many of them died.

It is nonetheless an effective technique for inducing a trance which some of us have tried. There are two ways of doing this. One is a heavy rhythmic beat that is not particularly painful but induces drowsiness leading to out-of-body experiences if persisted with long enough: we are talking hours. The other is a sharper beat that induces a stinging pain. The body's reaction to this is to tighten up, which constricts the cords around the throat, leading to slight asphyxiation which can produce the required trance.

Neither technique was used in the covens to which I have belonged – even in Gardner's time – or with whom I have guested. Afraid of showing the slightest aggression towards a fellow Craft member, the scourgers have applied such gentle strokes that the scourgee could barely feel and which were more like tickling than true scourging.

This completely symbolic scourging could up to a point be justified at the 1st degree initiation, as demonstrating that the trust the initiate displayed in allowing himself to be bound would not be misused. But it is completely useless as a method of purifying the mind from extraneous thoughts during the opening of the circle, or for inducing any sort of a trance.

Because of changing mores few people in the younger generations have fond memories of being spanked as a child by their mother or a pretty young governess and few are therefore into sado-masochistic practices. Some may on the contrary have traumatic memories of being physically abused by a brutal father. But those for whom this is not the case should at least try this method properly to see if it works. If it doesn't lift them out of present reality they should drop it and try one or more of the other methods for going into trance.

But the idea that anything is achieved with a symbolic scourging that is barely felt is self-deception on a grand scale and turns Wiccan rituals into a liturgy instead of a means to achieve ego-transcendence. It gives, us in the eyes of outsiders, the dubious reputation of being an S & M cult, but without any of the spiritual and sensual advantages that we might enjoy if we really were one.

THE GREAT RITE

Ritual sexual intercourse in the circle – not necessarily in front of other coven members – is supposed to play a major role at the 3rd degree elevation, which permits a newly elevated high priestess to hive off and form her own coven. If she has transcended her ego and identifies wholly with the Goddess she should be able to celebrate the Sacred Marriage with any Wiccan priest who had likewise transcended his ego and identified wholly with the Horned God.

But there's the rub. I know no Wiccan priestess who has transcended her own ego to the extent that she is prepared to be intimate with a man with whom she hasn't already got a relationship. A Wiccan woman with no current partner may accept to be intimate with the initiating high priest, but not otherwise, and no high priestess whom I know would elevate a male coven member in this way unless she had an open relationship with her partner the high priest. In the 1950s most people were even more inhibited, and Gerald was in any case too old to get it up.

So Gerald invented the Great Rite in token. As Dayonis – who had a very open relationship with Jack Bracelin – described it to me: "He lay on top of me and recited some ritual words, and that was it!" This has become standard Gardnerian practice.

Alex Sanders got nearer the original intent by raising committed couples to the 3rd degree together. First the high priestess has a token Great Rite with the man being elevated, then the high priest with the woman. Then the whole coven except the couple retire into an adjacent room while the newly elevated couple do a real Great Rite in the circle. When they have completed it they ring a bell and the whole coven come back into the circle that has now been charged with the energy of the couple's Great Rite.

A few years ago there was a debate in some Wiccan magazines whether 3rd degrees given with a token Great Rite were valid. Some people including me argued that a Wiccan man or woman who would not perform the Great Rite with anyone but their regular partner had obviously not yet transcended their ego and should recognise this: hence the practice of allowing experienced 2nd degree priestesses to hive off and found their own coven in England.

I now think that both parties to the argument missed the point. The essence of the 3rd degree is not the Great Rite but the ability to transcend one's ego consciousness and experience cosmic consciousness. This should lead a high priestess to the ability to channel the Goddess when the Moon is drawn down on her. The Great Rite is one of several methods whereby this can be achieved, if Tantric meditation methods are used to delay the two orgasms until both partners have floated into cosmic consciousness: which may take several hours.

If they achieve success in this it doesn't matter whether the two partners are regular partners, or the high priestess with the man being elevated, or the high priest with the woman being elevated, although the chances of success will be much greater if the two partners feel passionately for each other. If they fail the 3rd degree elevation has not been achieved.

Conversely, a coven member of either sex who has achieved cosmic consciousness without practising the Great Rite with anyone, but using one of the other methods listed above for transcending the ego, should be accepted as a valid 3rd degree. For a would-be high priestess the test is: Can she channel the Goddess when the Moon is drawn down upon her?

III

A More Mystical and Nature Oriented Wicca

11

THE RELIGIOUS FRAMEWORK

How could the Goddess religion's framework and initiatory Wiccan rituals be altered to induce a greater awareness of Nature among the participants? Here are a few ideas with which existing covens could experiment to test their effectiveness.

A SEMI-BALANCED DUOTHEISTIC RELIGION

I have written *Goddess* religion rather than *Paganism*, because the latter has become a much broader umbrella term that covers also the revived ethnic religions like the Nordic Asatru, the Lithuanian Romuva and the Russian and Ukrainian Perun religions. These are still strongly patriarchal although their panthea also include goddesses, and their very conservative social and moral attitudes differ from those of Goddess worshippers.

Why do I write about the *Goddess* and not the *Goddess and Horned God* religion? As Gerald Gardner intended it and the Pagan Federation's third principle affirms, the religion is supposed to be properly balanced between the female and male aspects of divinity, but it hasn't turned out that way. All Wiccans and those non-initiated outer court worshippers like the members of the Fellowship of Isis (FoI) have a strong feeling for the Goddess and of Her presence in FoI or Wiccan circles, much less so for the Horned God. There is no ritual for Drawing Down the Sun on a coven's High Priest in the original Book of Shadows, although some covens may have added one, and a coven's leader must always be the High Priestess not the High Priest.

THE GODDESS

The Goddess, under whichever traditional names we call Her, represents the eternal Life-Force, and its ever recurring cyclicity of birth, growth, sexual union, reproduction, decline into old age, death and reincarnation into a new body with a blank slate for new experiences. She is a very conservative universal energy, who seeks forever to maintain existing equilibria and all plant and animal species just as they are, by giving them strong survival instincts, including intolerance for any mutations. Our remote ancestors in the Palaeolithic must have experienced Her very much as we do.

She represents a role model for women, which hasn't changed much since the dawn of history. Women who marry to have children have much the same tasks as in the Palaeolithic: make a comfortable home for husband and children, be it in a cave, a cottage, a castle, an urban apartment or a suburban house; look after the children when they come, and cook for the whole family unless there are servants or subsidiary wives to do these tasks.

For men the Goddess represents the idealised polar opposite, the projection of their inner *anima*, to which they can relate in rituals.

It is because these roles have changed so little that the Palaeolithic and Neolithic Mother Goddess speaks to both contemporary men and women so strongly once we decide to acknowledge and worship Her.

But the Goddess is more than a role model for women and the idealised mate for men. She is Nature and the Life-Force itself, and our best way of worshipping Her is to live healthier lives and to become more aware of the Nature that surrounds us.

SEASONAL FESTIVALS

If we want to reconnect with Nature we should like our Pagan ancestors be flexible from year to year in the timing of our seasonal festivals and let the state of Nature guide us, not any book. This may be difficult in the winter when halls have to be hired months in advance for large open Pagan festivals, but this doesn't apply in the spring, summer and autumn when we can meet out of doors.

If we live too far from farming land to observe the annual agricultural and animal rearing cycle, let us take the flowering of some plant as the trigger for a festival: say snowdrops for Imbolc and the mayflower for

Beltane. Those of us with gardens can also check when the temperature has become warm enough to sleep out of doors.

In the summer even city dwellers can take trips to the countryside to observe when the cereal, fruit or vine harvest is complete – depending on which is the region's main produce – to time our harvest festival accordingly. And wherever we live we won't have to walk far to find a park in which leaves are falling and dead branches are breaking off in the autumn to celebrate Samhain/Halloween.

If we want good weather, then best choose the weekend closest to the Full Moon after the event that triggers the festival, because that is when the chances of having a high pressure zone pass over us are greatest.

Ritual Roles

The seasonal festivals should also be closely connected to the phases of a human life. We already do so at **Yule**, that most Pagan of Christian festivals, when we celebrate the birth of a new solar year by making our children and our presents to them the main focus of the celebration.

At the **spring fertility** festival, whether the climate in which we live induces us to celebrate it at Easter, the beginning of May or mid-summer, the main roles should be played by young nubile couples who need not necessarily be a coven's high priest and high priestess, nor even necessarily in a strong relationship with each other outside the circle.

At the **Harvest** festival, be it in July, August or late September, the officiating high priestess should be a mother of several children, and the high priest her husband.

Finally, at Samhain or **Halloween** the oldest members of the coven or of the wider Pagan community should lead the ritual, representing respectively the Crone Goddess and the dying God of the Year. Such an allocation of ritual roles will encourage covens to have a large age spread in their membership.

The Rules of Sympathetic Magic

Although I haven't seen or heard of it being done, many Wiccans and other Pagans hark back wistfully to a time when young couples made love in the fields in spring time to encourage the fertility of the crops. One of these days some Wiccan coven will do it in the fields of some sympathetic farmer, but if so they should obey some elementary rules.

1. The fields concerned should have been cultivated entirely biologically and there should be no artificial fertilisers or pesticides in the soil.
2. The couples should all be fertile: i.e. no post menopausal women nor sterile old men.
3. They should all be prepared to have children themselves and thus not have any contraceptive chemical in the blood nor wear any mechanical contraceptive device. Copulation with contraceptives or by postmenopausal women would at best be unproductive; at worst it might actually sterilise the field.

CALLING THE QUARTERS

If the calling of the elements at the four quarters is to put us truly in touch with them, then the high priestess and the coven as a whole should relax before opening a circle, and try to sense from which direction the energy associated with each element is coming most strongly. For those who have not yet attained sufficient sensitivity to do this, here is a rough rule of thumb: start with the densest element, Earth, and work your way up to the progressively finer elements: Water, Fire and finally Air.

To locate **Earth**, look around you if there is a visible mountain range from where you are; if there is, that is where you place Earth. If you are in a flat countryside with no local hills or mountains, then work out in which direction lies the greater part of the land mass on which the coven finds itself.

To locate **Water**, look around you if there is a large body of water close by or, failing this, a flowing river. If you cannot see one, work out in which river a drop of water would flow that you had just dropped in the middle of the planned circle, and into which sea or ocean that river then flows.

Put **Fire** in whichever direction the sun is at the time of your ritual if it takes place by day. If it takes place at night, choose the direction of the midday sun or – if that direction has already been taken – the rising sun.

Air, which is all around us, then takes up the last remaining direction, but you will be surprised how often that is from where most of the winds come.

Now if you use this system, you see how the Golden Dawn attributions, which most Wiccans use, originated: in south-west England or Wales. From there the greater part of the island of Great Britain is to the north, the Bristol Channel or Atlantic Ocean to the west, the midday Sun to the south, leaving the east for Air. For the Navajo of

New Mexico, on the other hand, the Rocky Mountains are west, the Gulf of Mexico south, the rising sun east, leaving north for Air.

When I lived in London, I used to go to a nearby wood most evenings, draw a circle on the ground and commune with the elements and the spirits of the wood. One day it occurred to me that a drop of water from where I stood would flow into the Thames which flows east into the North Sea. So I started invoking Water in the east and Air in the west – from where most of the Atlantic winds come, incidentally – and I immediately got a much stronger feeling of each of the four elements. Whenever I invoked Air in the west, a small breeze would blow in my face, a message from the air elementals that they were present.

When I proposed this system a few years ago in the American Wiccan magazine *The Hidden Path* a Virginian HPS wrote in to say: "I am a Wiccan, not a geographer! *I don't want to have to think* in which directions the four elements lie every time I draw a circle!" not an effective way of getting closer to Nature. She then went on to put this poser to me: "There is a small pond just north of my house, a river 10 miles to the west and the Atlantic Ocean 30 miles to the east. From which direction should I then call Water?" To which I replied: "You decide! Of which of these three bodies of water are you most conscious when you draw a circle in your garden: from where do you sense the water energy to come most strongly?"

THE HORNED GOD

Why doesn't the Horned God icon or energy speak to most of us as strongly as the Goddess? As the complement of the Goddess as Life-Force He should be the Supreme Identity, the point in time in an ocean of eternity. He should also be a role model for men to bring back the wherewithal with which to feed the family.

There's the rub. While the role of women in the family has hardly changed down the millennia, men's as breadwinners has. The Horned God is a hunting god, a role model for Palaeolithic hunters who went out in groups to stalk and hunt deer, bison and other horned animals, and bring their carcasses back to the family table for the wives to cook. But few of us are hunters any more: we earn our livings as engineers, computer programmers and operators, managers, salesmen, factory workers, doctors, psychotherapists or shopkeepers in our highly complex industrial civilisation, and to these modern tasks the Horned God has little to say.

At best the Horned God still represents the male lust that seeks out the female to impregnate her and perpetuate life. At some Wiccan gatherings invocations of *Io Pan* have ended up as sexual orgies. A good role model then for men to overcome our sexual inhibitions and be more imaginative in our lovemaking, but not in our professional lives.

THE GOD OF DEATH AND RESURRECTION

The same is even truer of the God of Death and Resurrection. As god of the underworld ruling the winter months he is in a polarity relationship with the Goddess seen as ruling the fertile spring, summer and autumn months. Together they rule the wheel of the year and preserve existing species in an eternal life cycle, but they do not account for Evolution nor for our modern scientific and technological civilisation.

Lacking a divine role model for industrial and commercial work, many Wiccans and other Goddess worshipping Pagans have dropped out of administrative, industrial and commercial jobs. Those with artistic creative talent can still earn their living making robes and jewellery; those with insight as psychotherapists; others drift. It is remarkable that despite this a majority of Wiccans still manage to make a valuable contribution to society, especially in the computer industry.

PROFESSIONAL PATRON GODS

To what other deity could those of us in industry or commerce relate better and invoke when we need more courage and inspiration? In the Greek pantheon *Hermes*, patron god of communication and commerce, is the ideal deity to preside over the Internet, the computer industry and all forms of commerce, while *Hephaistos* could inspire engineers and factory workers, *Asclepios* the medical profession, and they must have their equivalents in other pantheons.

Then why haven't they already been adopted? They would be valuable as professional patron deities which would sacralise our everyday jobs just as they did in antiquity. But they are not on a par with the Eternal Mother Goddess of Life and the Earth and could not be considered as consorts for Her. They are too partial for that, comparable to the minor goddesses that also represent partial aspects of the divine feminine: in the Greek pantheon *Kore, Aphrodite, Artemis, Hera, Demeter, Persephone* and *Hekate.*

THE GOD OF CREATION

The only universal energy worthy to look the Mother Goddess in the eye as an equal is the God of **Destructive Creation**, the dynamic power behind Evolution, who seeks forever to upset existing equilibria in order to force at least some of the existing species to become more highly evolved in order to survive. In a universe in which the total amount of energy is constant and can neither be added to nor reduced – although it can be converted to matter and back again – neither god nor man can create anything without destroying something else. This is the power the Jews call JHVH, the Christians God the Father, Muslims Allah and Hindus Shiva, and who has also been called Reason, History (by the Marxists) and the Market.

As I described it in the brainstorm I had in March 1957 until some 150 000 years ago the Destructive Creative force acted mainly from outside the Earth through asteroid impacts or sunspots and sunstorms that altered climates on Earth, destroying those species unable to adapt and giving an opportunity to others. This justifies to some extent the Christian theological view that the Creator is a *transcendent* power separate from His creation.

But these were crude methods of which the Destructive Creative force grew tired So it entered the left-hand side of the human brain and sought to use humanity as its instrument of creation and transformation on Earth – "making Man in His own image" in the words of Genesis – an event described in the Old Testament as the moment when Eve and Adam ate the fruit of the Tree of Knowledge, and which occurred in history when mankind learned to handle fire – the great destructive and transformative element – instead of just fearing it like all other animals.

Humanity, Microcosm of the Universe

But human beings, like all species, are still bound to existing equilibria by our powerful instincts, especially the power of Love for the environment in which we were born and in which we grew up, as well as for our parents, mates and children, whom we love just as they are and whom we wouldn't have otherwise. The power of Creation thus had to fight every inch to broaden its power over the human mind, and to alienate humanity from its essentially conservative instinctual drives. The eternal cosmic struggle between Love and the Destructive Creative Power thus entered the human soul, which became a microcosm of the Universe.

That is why, after centuries in which the ancient priesthoods kept the two forces in balance, the Persian prophet Zoroaster and a number of Jewish prophets beginning with Moses were inspired to proclaim the God of Creation the *only* God and to forbid the worship of all other deities, including the Great Mother Goddess of Life and Love.

It took centuries. Time and again the patriarchal monotheistic message syncretised with an existing Mother Goddess religion to form semi-balanced religions in which the Goddess is represented, albeit in a subordinate position. The most recent ones were Roman Catholic and Orthodox Christianity in which the Virgin Mary plays the same psychological role among worshippers as the various goddesses did in antiquity, especially Nuit and Isis.

The only truly monotheistic religions in which the God of Creation is worshipped to the exclusion of all others are Islam, Reformed and Liberal Judaism, and in the past 500 years Protestant Christianity.

A False God?

Just as patriarchal monotheists call other deities false gods created as human thought forms, so we Pagans have returned the compliment and called JHVH a false god, a thought form of Moses to make the Israelite men despise women and their feelings and become more warlike. How could a god who gave genocidal orders to the Israelites, and sent his "only" son to incarnate and let himself be crucified to reclaim humanity's sins, be a true deity!

But who says that gods must necessarily be gentle and loving? They are primal energies with their own agendas, who use their worshippers for their own ends.

A deity whose exclusive worship allowed the Jews to retain their collective identity through nearly two millennia of living without a land of their own as minorities among often very hostile peoples, and who has spurred the Protestant-dominated countries of Northern Europe and North America to create in under 500 years the most scientifically curious and technologically inventive civilisation that the world has ever known, is an awesome primal power with whom we ought to engage. A power moreover that still dominates the Western world and increasingly the developing countries as well.

A God on the Wane?

Don't be deceived by the decline in Christian belief and practice in the past 50 years, especially in Western Europe, where only some 11% of the population go to Christian Church services. We all know that the force of Destructive Creation doesn't mind whether it is called Shiva, JHVH, God the Father or Allah; but neither does it mind being called *Reason* (with a capital R as many Enlightenment theologians did and atheist philosophers do), *History* (with a capital H as the Marxists did) or the *Market*.

Few if any cathedrals are built in contemporary Western Europe and North America but plenty of commercial skyscrapers, which like the mediaeval cathedrals reach out to the sky and away from the despised Earth. And when men and women work five days a week and up to 10 hours a day in research laboratories, oil drilling platforms, factories, marketing or management, the Destructive–Creative force which they thereby serve doesn't mind if they don't go to synagogue on Saturday or church on Sunday. However, the United States, where over 70% of the people attend church on Sunday, is economically much more dynamic and technologically more inventive.

Engaging with the Creator God

Engaging with this power does not mean we should worship Him and give Him our individual spiritual power: too many Jews, Christians, Muslims and Rationalists do so already. Nor should we join in Jewish synagogue, Christian church or Muslim mosque services, too many of which implicitly or explicitly deny other deities, including the Great Mother Goddess: whether it is the Catholic and Anglican Nicean Creed: "I believe in *One* God, the *Father* Almighty...", or the Muslim "There is no God but God...". But we should meditate on Him and His symbols to get to know Him better and celebrate Him in collective festivals that we have designed ourselves.

113

Symbols

The main symbol of the Destructive and Creative God is the upward pointing arrow reproduced in the spire of Christian cathedrals and the commercial skyscrapers that celebrate the Market. Others might include measuring devices including clocks and watches, and monetary symbols for commercial exchange.

Festivals

We could dedicate the ever regular solar solstice and equinox festivals to the Destructive and Creative God. Alternatively or in addition we could celebrate the main inventions that have shaped Western technological society: steam power, electricity, the telephone and the computer, either on the day of the year on which each of them was announced or on the birthday of their inventor.

THE SACRED MARRIAGE

Having thus familiarised ourselves in our own way with and penetrated the Creator God's current, we should then in our minds and hearts bring Him to the altar of Our Lady the Goddess to marry Her in a true Sacred Marriage. This may seem a tall order, since from the dawn of time the relationship between the two deities has been one of opposition, punctuated by occasional violent rapes of the Earth Mother Goddess by the God of Creative Destruction, which have become quasi-permanent since the beginning of the Industrial Revolution.

But what choice do we have? Whether we like it or not the God of Destructive Creation is embodied in the left-hand side of our Pagan brains just as he is in the left-hand side of Jewish, Christian, Muslim and Rationalist brains. To ignore Him is to reduce ourselves to impotence in the struggle for the survival of life on Earth. The only way to cope with this is to acknowledge the God of Creation as a part of ourselves, and then set out to domesticate him in the service of our Lady of Life and Love.

The fact that throughout history patriarchal warrior religions of conquerors have syncretised with the polytheistic Nature religions of conquered people to produce balanced or semi-balanced duotheistic or polytheistic religions, shows that it can be done.

114

A symbol of this could be the penetration of the circle of Eternity and womb of the Mother Goddess by the upward pointing arrow symbolising the linear view of Evolution and history, but which would thereby also be contained and thus restrained: a more effective symbol than the usual male/female fertility symbols: the pentagram and hexagram. I leave to more creative people than myself the task of designing rituals to express this principle.

PRACTICAL RESULTS

The mundane result of such a true balanced duotheistic worship would be that those of us who do so will cease to drop out from our technological civilisation and reduce ourselves to impotence, even while keeping our hands clean. We would gladly accept scientific, engineering and managerial positions in contemporary industry and commerce, but use the power and influence these would give us to bend the industries in which we work to doing the Goddess' work: preserving and enhancing our ecological environments instead of putting them at risk with dangerous techniques of chemical and nuclear research and genetic manipulation.

12

AN INITIATORY PATH

Within the broader Goddess and Horned God religion Wicca (as defined in Europe) is an initiatory mystery cult and priesthood. One enters it through a formal initiation into a coven.

THE MEANING OF INITIATION

"In-itiation" includes the syllable "in". It is a ceremony in which a closed and secretive group admits an *out*sider and makes him into a group *in*sider. It is thus only meaningful when used by groups. The term "self-initiation" popularised by Scott Cunningham in his book *Wicca: a Guide Book for the Solitary Practitioner* is a misuse of the language. A solitary worshipper of the Goddess and/or Horned God can *dedicate* him or herself to his or her deities, who may respond and help him or her to grow spiritually and protect him or her in their lives, but he or she cannot self-initiate: into what?

Mass initiations at the end of a seminar on Wicca, such as Alex Sanders practised in Germany in the 1980s, are equally nonsensical if these do not admit the new initiates into working covens.

In Germany all Goddess worshippers call themselves Wiccan, whether initiated or not, to distinguish themselves from the Asatruar or practitioners of the Nordic religion who have appropriated the name *Heide,* the German word for both Pagan and Heathen. Most of these "Wiccans" live too far apart to be able to form covens, but will travel once every three months to celebrate a seasonal festival with other Wiccans from all over Germany.

After years of doing this uninitiated, some will ask an initiated 2nd or 3rd degree Wiccan to initiate them, and will then continue just to attend large seasonal festivals with the other Goddess worshippers as before. What purpose can such an initiation serve?

Initiation is not the Wiccan equivalent of the Christian baptism: it is a much too heavy a ritual for that. It includes a rite of rebirth into a coven, which will leave the new initiate utterly bereft if there isn't thereafter a coven she or he could attend regularly.

Esoteric religious groups are not the only ones to have formal initiation ceremonies for new members. Most American college fraternities and sororities have them, as do some faculties and academic establishments like the *École des Quatre Arts* in Paris and business fellowships like the Lions. Such ceremonies cement a strong feeling of group identity in the group into which one is thereby admitted.

Most initiatory ceremonies include a vow of *secrecy* about group activities towards outsiders, as well as an *ordeal*. An American academic who has studied fraternity and sorority initiation rituals has discovered that the more painful and/or humiliating the ordeal is, the greater will be the value that the initiate attaches to his membership of the group, and the greater will be the members' loyalty to the group and each other. Those Wiccan covens who have taken all pain out of our initiatory ordeal and reduced it to a symbolic ritual are not doing themselves or their initiates any favours. They mostly have little group cohesion and loyalty and tend to fall apart after a few years.

The Wiccan group into which one is initiated is a particular coven. The initiation does not confer on the initiate the right to attend any other coven's meetings unless specifically invited to do so. Least of all do "self-initiates" have the right to attend any coven's meetings unless they have previously submitted to that coven's initiation ritual.

THE CRAFT

There is little point in being initiated into any group unless that group has some exclusive knowledge or activity that outsiders do not share. In Wicca, the craft that we share includes:

- the ability to raise psychic power from within ourselves and to project it magically to empower a personal or group wish: mostly to heal someone or improve their fate;
- the ability to transcend our ego-consciousness and achieve cosmic consciousness.

Experienced witches and other magicians can raise psychic power and project it magically on their own, but newcomers can only safely learn it in a group. The inexperienced solitary practitioner can all too easily plunge more deeply into an altered reality than she or he can cope with, and might find it difficult to return to everyday reality if she or he has no experienced partner(s) or to help.

Like drugs the effectiveness of magical techniques is directly proportionate to their danger to the practitioner's sanity. Covens and magical lodges, on the other hand, have proven protection techniques and experienced members will recognise immediately if a new initiate has gone in too deeply and needs help.

A YEAR AND A DAY

According to Gerald Gardner's Book of Shadows at least a year and a day should elapse between an applicant's request to join a Wiccan coven and her or his initiation. When I applied to join Gerald Gardner's first coven the time was spent meeting the coven members socially prior to their meetings, so that we could get to know and trust each other. As I have mentioned above Gerald Gardner was so keen to have as many new initiates as possible that he gradually shortened this trial period.

There is, however, another reason for the year and a day waiting period which does not seem to have occurred to Gerald: it is a complete cycle of the seasons. If we want Wicca to become a true Nature-revering mystery cult, then applicants could be required to choose a corner of a wood or garden near their house in which they should spend half an hour a day to meditate and observe the changes in the appearance of the trees and other plants and of the behaviour of the animals from season to season. No need to await Halloween or Yule to begin the trial year: it could begin at any point in the year.

Psychically sensitive applicants might become gradually aware of the elemental spirits inhabiting individual plants and the wood as a whole. They would thus acquire a body of personal magical experience on the basis of which they could later evaluate what the coven teaches them after their initiation.

PRE-INITIATION TRAINING

Should covens have programmes of pre-initiation training? It depends on what sort of training is involved. If the coven teaches applicants to recognise different trees and plants by the shape of their leaves, and draws their attention to changes of their appearances from season to season, instead of leaving them alone to find this out for themselves, this can be quite valuable. So would courses on Wicca's exoteric religious framework, how we perceive the Goddess and the Horned God, and the leading Greek, Celtic and other ethnic myths.

However, the ring of secrecy surrounding the coven and helping to strengthen its group identity would be fatally weakened if inner ritual and magical techniques are taught applicants prior to their initiation into the group.

This is precisely what many contemporary Alexandrian and some Gardnerian covens do. In their pre-initiation training they often include ritual techniques for drawing circles, invoking the four quarters, as well as the construction of magical tools – all knowledge that should only be acquired after initiation.

Reading that at the end of the 1st degree initiation the initiate is proclaimed at the four quarters as "priest and witch", these Alexandrians interpreted "priest" in its usual Christian sense: as a man trained to perform religious rituals. Applicants therefore had to be trained in these before being initiated.

I share the opinion that to proclaim an initiate who as yet knows nothing of magical techniques a "priest and witch" is a bit overblown. But instead of adapting the words to the reality, these Alexandrians adapted the reality to what they perceived the words to mean, a witness to the superstitious awe in which words, especially written or printed words, can still be held.

Some Alexandrian covens and lines have, however, realised the undesirability of imparting secret ritual knowledge prior to initiation. They have therefore introduced an equally oathbound "Novice" degree into which their trainees are initiated before they are taught the main coven rituals and symbols, while still leaving the "1st degree" initiation to the end of their training.

An equally undesirable practice is that of at least one Gardnerian coven that I know: inviting applicants to share a circle with the coven when celebrating a seasonal festival at which no magic is performed. It is true that seasonal festivals are exoteric and not oathbound. But there is every difference between participating in an open festival with some 50 or 100 other participants, or sharing with the members of a coven a bonfire party, and joining a coven in a circle before one has been initiated. The latter means being in the circle without having been formally admitted: the applicant picks up some if not all the group's collective energy before the formal admission that the initiation is meant to represent, a recipe for spiritual confusion.

The justification for such pre-initiatory training in ritual techniques is that it allows the applicant to know what she or he is joining. But do any applicants move from coven to coven, or between Wiccan covens, Druid groves and Nordic henges, to sample their ritual techniques and then choose their coven on that basis?

Surely the only important criterion of choice is the empathy an applicant feels with a particular group of people: does she or he like and trust them and they her or him? Is their group energy right for him or her, or too weak or too intense? Do they appear to have knowledge she or he would find valuable? Meeting socially in pubs or around a bonfire is quite adequate for this purpose without learning which way around the coven draw pentagrams in the air for each of the four directions, or what magical tools they use to help them raise and direct power.

A lot of pre-initiatory training is an ego trip by the coven's high priestess or high priest to impose their conception of the Craft and its symbols on the applicant. The latter will then learn a lot of theory ahead of initiation and then compare his or her initiatory experience with what they had been taught to expect. Since Wicca is an experiential and not a dogmatic mystery cult, it is much better for an initiate to have the experience of the initiation first, which she or he can then use as the validation criterion for any theories she or he is later taught.

CROSS-GENDER INITIATION

Wicca assumes that most postulants will have been influenced by society's mores, and quite frequently repressed into conformity with them. These repress men's emotional side and boost their aggressive assertiveness, while they repress women's assertiveness and encourage them to be meek and submissive in a "feminine" way.

Each gender is thus crippled differently by society, and has to learn from the other gender what she or he is missing in their character. This is symbolised by the Wiccan practice of cross-gender initiation. Male postulants are thus always initiated by the High Priestess: they are thus put on notice that they will have a lot to learn from the women in the group, notably to be more tolerant and intuitive, and are "plugged" magically into the strong but gentle Goddess current.

Women postulants are initiated by the High Priest and "plugged" into the Horned God current, which will help them in time to gain in self-confidence and assertiveness.

As men and women initiates become less repressed and more balanced between the receptive and assertive parts of our character, we also gain in self-confidence to follow our true wills, irrespective of social pressures.

This applies of course mainly to heterosexual applicants to a mixed gender coven. Gay and lesbian covens will have to find their own way to balance their energies within themselves and between each other. It would presumably be a matter of matching an assertive high priest(ess) with a gentler more receptive applicant and vice versa.

I don't think "renting a priestess" from another coven just for initiations and elevations, in the manner of the New York gay men's coven, would achieve very much apart from ensuring their position in the Gardnerian lineage. Balancing energies cannot be achieved in a simple initiation ceremony: it requires continuous example and training in subsequent coven meetings, which a "rented priestess" would be unable to do in a gay men's coven.

Some "politically correct" Eclectic covens deny any inherent character differences between men and women and thus see no need for initiations to be cross-gender. The psychological results can be disastrous. A few years ago I met a German Wiccan man who had been initiated by another man. Far from being balanced by his initiation his male assertive side had been potentiated and he had received no balancing gentle side. He was very dogmatic and ran a trainee coven of people of both genders in a very authoritarian way. After a few months his trainees left him and reformed a trainee coven of their own without him. He then sent a letter to all the Wiccan covens whom he knew asking them to refuse admission and initiation to any of the trainees who had deserted him, a request which they all ignored. Years later he was still writing to his former trainees asking them for their reasons for leaving him.

13

THE THREE DEGREE PARADIGM

There are three degrees of initiation in Wicca, as in most Freemason lodges, who in turn took this system over from the mediaeval craft guilds. Indeed, like the Freemasons, we tend to call our tradition "the Craft" among ourselves.

The craft guilds governed all our trades and early industry for centuries. Their three degree system – apprentice, journeyman, master – is thus a very powerful paradigm, which we must understand to work it effectively, even though the three Wiccan degrees also differ in some respects.

In the Middle Ages, when a boy (it usually was a boy) wanted to become say a baker, his parents would approach a master baker in the same city and ask him to take him on as *apprentice*. If the master baker accepted, then at some time between the ages of 11 and 15 the boy would leave his parents' home and move into the master baker's house and become to all intents and purposes a member of his family.

Up to that point he knew what bread and cakes were since he had eaten them in his parental home, but he would not know how they were made. It is only after he had become a member of the master baker's family that he would gradually learn the baker's guild trade secrets. In Wicca we should follow this practice.

The young apprentice would have to obey his master in all things and watch him at work at all the hours when this was necessary, including getting up at 4 a.m. to light the ovens to bake the bread that customers would be buying fresh from 7 a.m. onwards; or serving in the shop. As he learned the craft of bread baking, he would be gradually entrusted with small and then bigger tasks. At first, it might be just serving in the shop. Later, he might be trusted to bake the morning bread on his own. Finally, he would be taught how to buy different types of flour, how to recognise good from bad, how to haggle about the price.

When the master baker regarded his young apprentice as fully competent in all that he could teach him, he would formally raise him to the status of *companion* or *journeyman* baker, usually between the ages of 18 and 21. He would now be entitled to be paid a wage for his work in the bakery. Mostly, however, he would now leave his master's employ and travel to other cities, sometimes to other countries throughout Europe. In each city he visited, he would seek work with a local master baker, and learn his way of baking bread and cakes, which would vary from city to city and, of course, from country to country as it still does today.

After 10 to 12 years' travelling in this way, when the journeyman baker felt he had learned all he could about the art of baking bread throughout England or Europe, he would return to the city of his birth and the bakery where he had first learned his trade. There, under the guidance of his original master, he would in his spare time work on his *masterpiece*: the most artistic and tasty loaf of bread or cake that he was capable of making. At the next bakers' guild festival, he would present his masterpiece to all the assembled master bakers of the city.

If the masterpiece passed muster, its author would then be ceremoniously raised to the status of *master* baker. He would now be entitled to marry – frequently the daughter of his original master – to open his own baker's shop, employ journeymen and take on apprentices of his own. The same procedures were followed in all other craft guilds.

Wiccan initiation and the two subsequent elevations to the 2nd and 3rd degrees should follow this paradigm fairly closely. The main differences are that men and women are initiated equally, and are always a great deal older at their 1st degree initiation: the minimum age is 18.

Since the release of the film *The Craft* and the magical TV sitcoms *Buffy*, *Charmed* and *Sabrina* there has been a great increase in teenage interest in witchcraft, but pressure to lower the minimum initiation age should be resisted. Teenagers, especially girls, have quite enough on their plate coping with increased hormonal activity during puberty without having the added pressure of the accelerated spiritual growth that can follow an initiation.

There is no reason, however, why teenagers should not be admitted to open seasonal festivals with their parents' permission, nor why they should not be admitted to outer court non-initiatory organisations like the Children of Artemis or the UK Pagan Federation.

Some Wiccans have suggested adding a fourth or fifth degree: none of these systems would have the morphic resonance of the mediaeval three degree system.

FIRST (APPRENTICE) DEGREE

The craft that a 1st degree apprentice witch learns within her or his coven is the ability to raise and control psychic power from within her or himself and to contribute it to the coven's collective energy when working a group spell. She or he should also cultivate under the high priestess' guidance whatever psychic potential she or he has, be it divination, astral travel or any other.

Title

In the Gardnerian Book of Shadows the new initiate is proclaimed "Priest and Witch" at the four quarters at the end of the 1st degree initiation. Gerald, or his initiator in the New Forest coven, probably intended this to mean that initiates are plugged in from their first initiatory circle into the Goddess' and Horned God's current, and can communicate with them directly, which priests and shamen do in all cultures. But as we have seen in the case of many covens, it is a title that can all too easily be misinterpreted as implying ritual competence and thus requiring a great deal of pre-initiatory training.

It seems to me more appropriate, therefore, if the new initiate were proclaimed more modestly "Apprentice Priest and Witch". The proclamation at the four quarters might run like this: "Take heed, ye mighty spirits of Air/Fire/Water/Earth, guardians of the portals of E/S/W/N, _____ (name) has been apprenticed to the _____ coven to learn the Craft of the Priest and Witch."

After this formal initiation ritual, the new apprentice witch learns the coven's magical knowledge and techniques by doing: participating in group spells and other work and contributing her or his power to them.

During her or his apprenticeship she or he should only circle with the coven into which she or he has been initiated and not practise any other magical or meditation discipline concurrently to avoid spiritual confusion.

Magical Tools

In the Gardnerian tradition the 1st degree initiate's main task is to build his or her own magical tools, although even in Gerald's day it was allowed to buy one's tools and just add the appropriate magical symbols on them. This is once again putting too much importance on symbolism.

In my opinion, initiates should first be taught to project power with the upraised second and third fingers of the right hand (or left hand for left handed people). Only afterwards should they learn how to use the different tools to invoke the elemental energy that the tool represents; and only when they have learned this to start fashioning their own personal tools.

Gerald Gardner did not tell us that each of the magical tools symbolises one of the four alchemical elements, which is well known in other magical traditions. There are personal tools as well as coven tools (not weapons!).

Element	Personal tool	Coven tool
Air	Athame, white-handled knife	Sword
Fire	Wand, scourge(?)	Broom, censer
Water	Cup, mirrors	Chalice, cauldron
Earth	Plate	Stone

Since in the 1st degree initiates learn how to raise and project their own personal energy, only the personal tools should be presented during the 1st degree initiation, and they should be properly balanced between the four elements. As I have mentioned in a previous chapter Gerald Gardner's prescription of presenting the sword, athame and white-handled knife at 1st degree initiation over-emphasises the element of Air and therefore the intellect, while the omission of the cup devalues the element of Water, and the feelings that this represents. Presenting the sword – a coven tool – should be left to the 2nd degree elevation, while I see no need to have a white-handled knife separate from the athame.

Country witches use ordinary household implements as their magical tools, and would use their kitchen knife as their athame. To reserve magical tools solely for circle work – and having a white-handled knife separate from the athame to fashion one's tools – is a hangover from ceremonial magic and the dualist separation of the sacred from the profane.

Wicca is supposed to be a monist pantheist mystery cult, in which initiates learn to see the whole of life as divine, and all everyday activities as equally sacred. Consequently the athame could very well be used also for fashioning one's magical tools and even for preparing a meal.

There is, however, a very good reason for magical tools to remain private to their owner and not to be used by anyone else, so they can become imbued only with their owner's vibrations.

Athame. In the Book of Shadows Gerald Gardner describes the athame as "the true witch's weapon." I disagree on two counts. First of all, we should not talk of "weapons", which implies that the nature around us is essentially hostile and we have to defend ourselves against it. This was presumably the attitude of Renaissance magicians, who shared with the Christian church a negative view of Nature. But Wicca is a mystery cult for reconciling humanity, and in the first place its own initiates, with Nature and we should not therefore approach it with "weapons" but only with "tools" if we need these at all.

The athame is a useful tool when working indoors to draw a circle as a magical boundary between the everyday world and the magical inner world. But as the experience that I described in chapter 5 proved, elemental spirits fear all iron and steel tools. Therefore both athame and sword should always be left at home when working out of doors and seeking the company and help of Nature spirits. An athame made of crystal or stone would probably not have such a bad effect on elemental spirits

The only time a country witch would have taken a consecrated knife with her out of doors would have been when cutting medicinal herbs with their mother plants' permission.

Wand. In my opinion a truer witch's tool is the wand, which can be used both in the house and out in the open to symbolise and extend the witch's magical will. Gerald Gardner admits this in the Book of Shadows when he writes: "This is used to summon certain spirits with whom it would not be meet to use the athame." Certain spirits? Yes, all Nature spirits!

Scourge. I am not sure to which element the scourge belongs, but since it is an instrument for exercising power over others it probably belongs to Fire.

Cup. The cup symbolises receptivity, and especially emotional openness to all the joys and sorrows that life brings us. It is in my opinion the most important tool for any Goddess worshipper, except that many Wiccans would not describe it as a tool, but as the Craft's central mystery, symbolising the Goddess' womb.

Magical mirrors. The Gardnerian BoS makes no reference to magical mirrors, another indication that Gerald Gardner never met any country witches. But according to the late Cecil Williamson, the founder and former owner of the Witches' Museum at Boscastle in Corn-wall, all country witches had two magical mirrors. They used a *black* backed mirror for scrying as an alternative to looking into the cauldron filled with water. If a witch looked intently into it her own reflection would gradually mutate into the face of her own guardian spirit, who would answer her questions or inform her of developments on the astral plane that she should know.

The other mirror would be *silver* backed and used for protection. Any witch thinking that she faced a magical attack would draw a protective circle around her house with the silver backed mirror facing outwards, so that any hostile or otherwise negative energies were sent straight back to from where they came. The following spell came to me for consecrating a silver backed protective mirror, and I happily share it with you:

> "Silver backed mirror of the art,
> Protect me in the Lady's name,
> Save me from sorrow, save me from shame,
> Send hateful thoughts back whence they came
> (Magnified three fold in her name)*
> Let only love through to my heart!"

Obviously, when one is receiving negative thoughts from a person one has wronged it would be better to make it up with the wronged person rather than using the mirror's protection, but there are situations where there is no other way.

If the mirrors as well as the cup are presented at 1st degree initiation that might be overemphasising the element of Water in the same way as Gerald overemphasised Air with the presentation of the sword, athame and white-handled knife. Alternatively, presenting several Water tools could be balanced by presenting several knives after all to represent Air.

Plate. In the Bricket Wood coven, every member had his or her personal plate engraved with a magical symbol, and on which she or he put the consecrated mooncakes (during Cakes & Wine) or other food eaten in the circle. It is important that a plate be also presented to a new initiate so as to maintain a balance between all the four elements in the tools presented.

Overcoming addictions

In my opinion controlling one's own power should also involve overcoming any physical or chemical addictions that one may have, be

---

Note: * That line is optional and should only be used when under deliberate malignant attack.

it alcoholism, chain smoking or any other form of drug dependency, as well as psychological compulsions like excessive eating, excessive surfing on the Internet or excessive reading, when these are used to shield oneself from coping with everyday reality and relationships.

The 1st degree initiate should not be left to overcome these addictions and compulsions on her or his own, but be helped in this by the whole coven, and especially its high priestess and high priest.

THE 2ND (COMPANION) DEGREE

In the Middle Ages an apprentice who had become competent in all that his master had taught him would be raised to the status of *Companion* or *Journeyman*. This last term describes the practice of most journeymen of the time to leave their master's shop and travel around their country, often the whole of Europe, to learn other cities' and other countries' skills in baking bread or cakes, cobbling shoes, engraving jewellery or whatever trade the journeyman's was.

This is a practice we might well resurrect in Wicca. 2nd degree Wiccans are already allowed to guest with other covens, and some groups of covens often guest with each other and encourage their members to do so. But these are mostly closely related covens whose methods of working magic and organising seasonal rituals will differ little from each other.

More could be gained by guesting with Wiccan covens from a different line or in another country, if one's job enables one to travel. It was while guesting in the United States, 30 years after my initiation, that I learned to perform weather magic, while my American hosts were less adept at spiritual healing than my English mother coven had been.

Some adventurous spirits might even train in a different magical system such as the Kabbalah or Reiki or Yoga. They should be careful, however, to check that the world view and values of this other system are compatible with Wiccan values to avoid spiritual confusion. The most compatible and useful other magical traditions would be:

- Hindu **Tantra** to learn how to achieve cosmic consciousness with the Great Rite;
- **Voudun** or the Yoruban **Ifa Orisha** religion to learn how to achieve divine possession and thus channel gods and goddesses.

Or they might simply train in psychotherapy, alternative healing methods (e.g. homoeopathy, acupuncture) and group dynamics, which would stand them in good stead in later years when leading a coven of their own.

Many Wiccans may want to do their journeying before returning to their mother coven to learn the skills needed to lead a coven. This should be reflected in the 2nd degree elevation ritual, which might be divided into two parts not necessarily performed on the same night:

1. checking and acknowledging the apprentice's skills in controlling his or her own energy,
2. introduction to the training for High Priest(ess)ship.

The 2nd degree Elevation

In Chapter 2 I related how Gerald Gardner once told us: "Until recently witches were not allowed to write anything down, lest it incriminate them if their house was searched. When at last Books of Shadows were allowed, witches had to write their rituals and spells down in a jumbled manner, so that if any unauthorised person found the Book of Shadows and tried the rituals as written down they wouldn't work!" No ritual is more jumbled and intellectually confused than the Book of Shadows 2nd degree elevation ritual!

It starts logically enough with a 1st degree initiate requesting an elevation from the existing 2nd and 3rd degree members of his or her coven and showing the high priest(ess) the tools she or he has fashioned. But then the high priest(ess) presents these tools again to the initiate as in the 1st degree initiation: this doesn't make sense! It is the tools' owner who should present them to the coven's high priest(ess), and if need be ask the high priest(ess) to help him or her to consecrate them.

The high priest(ess) then asks the postulant to demonstrate her or his familiarity with the use of each tool. This is right. After all, the tools are just symbols of the various alchemical elements with which a witch may have to work, and the postulant should show the right competence in mastering the art of dealing with each element, both in his or her psyche and in the world around him or her.

When this has been done the first part of the ritual could be concluded with a presentation of the postulant to the four quarters with words such as: "Take heed ye mighty guardians of the portals of the E/S/W/N, elements of A/F/W/Ea, _____, an apprentice to the _____ coven, has become a fully competent Witch and Priest(ess) of the Great Goddess and Horned God, free to perform magic on her/his own and to journey to other covens and magical traditions!"

Training for Coven Leadership

The second part of the 2nd degree elevation ritual could be performed immediately or at a later date, but only when the postulant truly wishes to train as a future high priest(ess). It should begin with the reading of the Second Instruction (which some covens but not all have in their Book of Shadows), in which the postulant is warned that his or her training will involve channelling the Goddess or the Horned God, but that these are pure beings who do not tolerate any imperfections in their human vessels. Hence the importance of postulants having freed themselves from any addictions or compulsions or other avoidable weaknesses prior to their elevation.

Now should come the presentation by the high priest(ess) of the coven tools to the postulant, once again in a balanced manner, presenting not only the coven sword, stang or broom and censer of incense, but also the chalice, cauldron and stone. The high priest(ess) should demonstrate the use of each tool, thereby balancing the demonstration by the postulant of each of his or her personal tools earlier in the ceremony or at a past date.

After this would be an appropriate moment for the 3 times 40 stroke scourging laid down in the Gardnerian Book of Shadows, since any wrong decision by the high priest(ess) of a coven could rebound on her or him three times over or even more. If this is performed in a proper way with a slight sting or a heavy rhythmic beat, the postulant should be well on the way to an altered state of consciousness transcending his or her ego by the time the 120th stroke falls, which is after all what high priest(ess)ship is all about. Performed in the by now all too common light tickling manner it is embarrassingly boring for all concerned.

After this, the Gardnerian Book of Shadows lays down a reading and enacting the very moving Goddess' journey into the underworld and Her encounter with the Lord of Death and Resurrection. But since this journey concludes with the Sacred Marriage of the two it doesn't belong there but in the 3rd degree elevation, which is why Alexandrian covens almost always perform 2nd and 3rd degree elevations at the same time. Why not simply relegate this ritual to the 3rd degree elevation?

Similarly, it is only at the end of the 3rd degree elevation that a postulant should be proclaimed "High Priest(ess) and Witch Queen/Magus" at the four quarters, since it is only then that she or he is allowed to hive off from the coven and found a coven of her own.

The proper title that should be proclaimed at the four quarters should be something like: "Take heed, ye mighty guardians of the portals of the E/S/W/N, spirits of A/F/W/Ea, _____ a witch and priest of the Great Goddess and Horned God, has asked to be trained as a High Priest(ess) and coven leader."

This training should, as it now is, once again be on the job, during normal coven meetings, in which the coven's high priestess asks the trainee high priest(ess) to lead the coven in a spell or some other ritual.

THE 3RD (HIGH PRIEST(ESS)) DEGREE

A journeyman of a mediaeval craft guild had to present his masterpiece to the assembled masters of his guild in order to be raised to the status of Master himself, whereupon he could marry and open his own shop. A Wiccan priestess' masterpiece is the ability to enter into a trance at will and then channel the Goddess when the Moon is drawn down upon her during a coven meeting.

In the original Gardnerian Book of Shadows the 3rd degree elevation involves a Great Rite (ritual sexual intercourse between the coven high priestess and male coven member being elevated to the 3rd degree, or between the coven high priest and the woman member being elevated). Both the initiating high priest(ess) and the coven member being elevated should be the Goddess and the God in trance and as such be prepared to be sexually intimate with whoever was possessed by the complementary deity. This symbolises at the same time the Wiccan conviction that sexual intimacy between loving couples is the highest sacrament.

This has rarely happened during the past 50 years, because few if any high priest(esse)s and coven members being elevated were in the required trance and – in the absence of such a trance – few women were prepared to be intimate with anyone but their regular partner. So Gerald introduced the Great Rite in token, in which the high priest(ess) lies briefly on top of the coven member being elevated while reciting part of Crowley's Gnostic Mass, but without intromission.

At the time I was one of a small minority who argued that a refusal to be intimate with one's high priest(ess) meant that the person being elevated had not yet reached the level of spiritual development that the 3rd degree implied. Why not admit as much, and let experienced 2nd degree priestesses hive off and form their own covens, keeping the real Great Rite as the ritual for true 3rd degree elevation? But this was very much a minority viewpoint, and most would be high priest(esse)s were happy to be elevated with a token Great Rite.

A small number of Gardnerian covens in England and California perform real Great Rites between the high priest(ess) and coven member being elevated, whether these are actually in trance or not. This intimacy creates strong emotional bonds between the high priest(ess) and coven member being elevated, which will weld all concerned into strong magical teams. Such bonds are no incentive to hiving off, however, so that while such covens endure for decades they have few if any daughter covens. In a modification of a saying about families "The covens who sleep together stay together."

Alex Sanders and his followers have pioneered an imaginative solution. They only raise committed couples together to the 3rd degree – usually immediately after their 2nd degree elevation and the journey into the underworld. First the woman has a token Great Rite with the high priest, then the man has a token Great Rite with the high priestess. Then high priestess, high priest and the other 3rd degree members of the coven (who alone are allowed to attend) leave the room and the couple can perform a real Great Rite on their own in the middle of the circle, which they thereby charge with Sacred Marriage energy. When they have finished they ring a bell and those waiting outside can return to the circle. Or else the couple close the circle and rejoin the rest of the coven in the sitting room.

This restricts hiving off to committed 3rd degree Wiccan couples, which is a very good idea. Covens headed by a committed couple tend to last as long as the high priestess' and high priest's relationship, and since the HPS/HP couple ideally meet each other's emotional needs, the high priestess is less likely to go on an authoritarian ego trip.

A Tantric Great Rite

It seems to me now that both the proponents and the opponents of the token Great Rite had missed the point. The Great Rite is not an end in itself but one of several means whereby a would-be high priestess and high priest can enter into a trance and channel the Goddess and the Horned God. A mere adulterous fuck won't achieve anything. It should be a prolonged tantric union in which both parties defer orgasm almost indefinitely until they jointly float into an altered state of consciousness in which they truly are the Goddess and the God, as I did with my first lover $2\frac{1}{2}$ years before being initiated into Wicca.

If a couple can achieve such a mystical identification with the divine couple then it doesn't matter whether they already are a committed couple, or the high priestess coupling with a male coven member being elevated, or the high priest with a female coven member. If they don't achieve this then they have failed whatever combination of people is involved. In all cases, therefore, there should be a great deal of private practice before attempting this within a ritual circle during a 3rd degree elevation.

According to Hindu Tantric tradition it is impossible for a man to achieve such ego-transcendence in the arms of his wife, but only with a temple priestess, but that is because traditional Hindu marriages are arranged by parents, and the partners hardly ever feel passionate about each other. Western couples who are allowed to marry for love can feel passionate about each other, which is a prerequisite for being able to jointly transcend their egos into divine consciousness.

A Suggested 3rd Degree Elevation Ritual

Only the coven's high priestess. High priest, other 3rd degree coven members if any, and the postulant(s) should be present. After the circle has been properly opened, the God of Death and Resurrection is called down upon the male postulant, if any, and the Moon is called down upon the woman postulant. The Goddess' descent into the underworld is then read out and enacted by the couple. When she declares her love for the God, the high priestess (unless she is the Goddess), the high priest (unless he acts as the God) and other 3rd degree members withdraw from the circle and the room and leave the couple to enact their Tantric coupling.

When the couple have returned sufficiently into present time to ring the bell and summon those waiting outside back in, the entranced Goddess should be allowed to give spontaneous Goddess messages to those present, and the entranced God likewise. When they have thus demonstrated their ability to enter into trance and channel the Goddess and/or God, the high priestess wills all her power into the male postulant and the high priest all his power into the woman postulant. They are then presented to the four quarters as High Priestess and/or High Priest, empowered to found their own coven.

DRAWING DOWN THE MOON

It isn't just at her 3rd degree elevation that a new high priestess should be able to enter into trance and channel the Goddess, but whenever in her new coven the Moon is drawn down upon her. How can she enter into trance at will?

When a coven is run by a committed 3rd degree couple, they may want to charge their circle with a Tantric Great Rite on coven meeting evenings before the other coven members have arrived. But they will have to have descended from their trance in time to greet their other coven members, have a preliminary chat and then draw the circle and perform the circle opening ritual. Drawing down the Moon on the high priestess will occur later.

In principle, the high priestess should then channel the Goddess and give on Her behalf specific advice to the coven as a whole or to individual members. The Charge of the Goddess is a standby to be recited if the Goddess doesn't come through. But the Charge can also be used as a form of neurolinguistic programming to revive the high priestess' memory of her most recent trance.

The Charge as Neurolinguistic Programming

Compare the Charge with the *Manifestation of Isis* in Lucius Apuleius' *Golden Ass*. After She has appeared to Lucius She begins by introducing Herself as Nature, and then reciting all the Goddess names by which She was known at that time around the Aegean and the Mediterranean. Only after that long introduction does She get down to specifics and tell Lucius what he has to do to regain his human form.

The same sequence should be followed with the Charge. After the High Priest has called on the coven to "Listen to the Great Mother..." the High Priestess should omit the long paragraph "Whenever you have need of anything..." and wade straight into the self-introduction while strongly visualising what she is saying and recalling her most recent trance:

> "I am the Soul of Nature Who gives life to Universe,
> From Me all things proceed and unto Me all things must return.
> I am the beauty of the green Earth and the white Moon among
>   the stars,
> And the mystery of the waters and the desire in the heart of men.

I am the gracious Goddess Who gives the gift of joy unto the
heart of Man,
For Mine is the ecstasy of the Spirit, and Mine also is joy on
Earth,
For my law is love unto all beings.
Mine also is the secret door of youth and Mine is the cup of the
wine of life,
And the cauldron of Cerridwen which is the holy Grail of
Immortality."

Long before she has finished reciting this self-introduction the High
Priestess should be in a trance and be communicating the Goddess'
own specific advice to the coven. If, however, the Goddess doesn't
come through, the High Priestess can go on reciting the remainder of
the Charge, ending with:

"And thou who thinkest to seek for me . . ."

Even high priestesses who have never been in a trance or practised a
Tantric Great Rite might try this method: it might work.

CONCLUSION

This concludes my suggested modifications to Gardnerian and Alexandrian Book of Shadows rituals to make them more effective in bringing initiates of all three degrees closer to Nature, and enabling them to transcend their ego consciousness, achieve cosmic consciousness and full identity with the Goddess or the God at will. I have deliberately not rewritten any Book of Shadows rituals completely, both because these should remain oathbound and not accessible to the general reader, and to give my coven readers an opportunity to exercise their poetic creativity.

Obviously, if the current Book of Shadows rituals as they stand fulfil all your spiritual needs and achieve whatever you expect of them, then you have no reason to change them. But if they don't and you are left with a vague feeling that there is something missing, why not try out some of my suggestions. They are not an all-or-nothing system: pick out whatever suggestions you find most interesting, and any which you thought of yourselves, and try them out. And if they work better, do share your experiences with other covens to whom you are close.

The same goes for members of other Wiccan traditions, such as Dianics and Eclectics. Pick up any ideas you find interesting and applicable to your rituals and try them out.

And always remember: all rituals, be it those of the original Gardnerian Book of Shadows or the modified ones that I have suggested in this book, are but means to the end of ego transcendence and unity with the Mother Goddess and God, and should be judged by their effectiveness in achieving these ends.

BIBLIOGRAPHY

WICCAN HISTORY

Gerald B. Gardner. *Witchcraft Today*. Rider, London 1954.

Gerald B. Gardner. *The Meaning of Witchcraft*. London 1959.

Jack Bracelin. *Gerald Gardner, Witch*. Octagon Press, London 1960.

Ronald Hutton. *The Triumph of the Moon: A History of Modern Pagan Witchcraft*. Oxford Paperbacks 2001.

Philip Heselton. *Wiccan Roots. Gerald Gardner and the Modern Witchcraft Revival*. Capall Bann 2001.

Philip Heselton. *Gerald Gardner and the Cauldron of Inspiration*. Capall Bann 2003.

Doreen Valiente. *The Rebirth of Witchcraft*. Robert Hale, London 1989.

Lois Bourne. *Witch Among Us*. Robert Hale, London 1985.

Lois Bourne. *Conversations with a Witch*. Robert Hale, London 1996.

Lois Bourne. *Dancing with Witches*. Robert Hale, London 1998.

Patricia Crowther. *One Witch's World*. Robert Hale, London 1998.

Patricia Crowther. *High Priestess: The Life of Patricia Crowther*. Robert Hale, London 1999.

Patricia Crowther. *From Stagecraft to Witchcraft: The Early Years of a High Priestess*. Capall Bann 2001.

WICCAN PRACTICE

Janet and Stewart Farrar. *Eight Sabbats for Witches*. Robert Hale, London 1981.

Janet and Stewart Farrar. *The Witches' Way*. Robert Hale, London 1984.

Janet and Stewart Farrar. *Rituals: Witches' Bible*. Magickal Childe, 1987.

Janet and Stewart Farrar. *The Witches' Goddess: the Feminine Principle of Divinity*. Robert Hale, London 1987.

Janet and Stewart Farrar. *The Witches' God: the Masculine Principle of Divinity*. Robert Hale, London 1989.

Janet and Stewart Farrar. *Spells and How They Work*. Robert Hale, London 1990.

Janet and Stewart Farrar. *The Witches' Bible: the Complete Witches' Handbook*. Robert Hale, London 1996.

Janet Farrar and Gavin Bone. *Progressive Witchcraft: Spirituality, Mysteries and Training in Modern Wicca*. New Page Books 2003.

Tanya M. Luhrmann. *Persuasions of the Witch's Craft*. Blackwell, Oxford 1989.

Vivianne Crowley. *Wicca: the Old Religion in the New Age*. Aquarian 1989.

Vivianne Crowley. *Wicca. a Comprehensive Guide to the Old Religion in the Modern World*. Harper Collins 1996.

Vivianne Crowley. *The Magickal Life: a Wiccan Priestess Shares Her Secrets*. Penguin, London 2003.

Vivianne Crowley. *The Natural Magician: Practical Techniques for Empowerment*. 2003.

Vivianne Crowley. *Everyday Magic: Tap Your Natural Powers of Intuition*. Penguin, London 2004.

Patricia Crowther. *Lid off the Cauldron: Handbook for Witches*. Weiser, New York, 1985.

Frederic Lamond. *Religion without Beliefs: Essays in Pantheist Theology, Comparative Religion and Ethics*. Janus, London 1997.

CONTACTS

ORGANISATIONS

International
Pagan Federation International www.paganfederation.org

United Kingdom
Pagan Federation UK: www.paganfed.demon.co.uk
Children of Artemis: www.witchcraft.org

Belgium
Greencraft: www.greencraft.be

Germany
Pagan Federation DA.CH: www.pagan-federation.de

Austria
Wurzelwerk: www.wurzelwerk.at

North America
Covenant of the Goddess: www.cog.org
Pagan Federation USA: www.pfi-usa.org
Pagan Federation Canada: www.pfpc.ca

Brazil
Pagan Federation Brazil: www.br.paganfederation.org

South Africa
Pagan Federation of South Africa: www.pfsa.org.za

Australia

Pagan Federation of Australia: www.au.paganfederation.org

PUBLICATIONS

United Kingdom

Pagan Dawn: Pagan Dawn, BM Box 5896, London WC1N 3XX
The Pentacle: Pentacle, 78 Hamlet Road, Southend-on-Sea, Essex
The Cauldron: BM Cauldron, London WC1N 3XX
Witchcraft & Wicca: BM Artemis, London WC1N 3XX
The Wiccan: Box NWP, 70 Chestergate, Macclesfield, Cheshire
White Dragon: www.whitedragon.org.uk

Germany

Steinkreis: c/o Uta Sprenger, Puntheide 21, D-33619 Bielefeld

North America

NewWitch: www.newwitch.com
PanGaia: www.pangaia.com